A FULLY-LOADED LIFE

SPIRITUAL FRUIT: AN OUTFLOW OF AUTHENTIC CHRISTIAN LIVING

NEW INTERNATIONAL VERSION

PATIENCE
LOVE
GENTLENESS
SELF-CONTROL

JEREMY TULLIS

A Fully-Loaded Life Volume I- Spiritual Fruit
Copyright © 2004 by Antioch Media.

Requests for information should be addressed to:
Antioch Media
http://www.AntiochMedia.com/
438 E. Shaw Ave. #386
Fresno, CA 93710-7602

ISBN 0-9747772-1-8

Interior design by Antioch Media

Cover design by Josiah Micheletti and Ed Vinson

Printed in the United States of America

Contents

I hope that you are ready for an adventure over the next twelve weeks. Be ready for God to move in your life like never before. This devotional book will take you through the Spiritual Fruit needed to live a life that is totally on the edge for Christ. However, the ride does not stop there. In fact, in the final chapters, this book will take you through the action steps of applying the Spiritual Fruit. This book is a must to engage you to deepen your faith and love for Jesus.

Everyone loves movies. What better way to discover the truths of the Bible than through a movie format. This book has a simple, yet effective layout. Each chapter is broken up into seven, one-day increments. Each day is designed to give you depth without requiring much time. Let's get you familiar with the book's layout.

TRAILER
The trailer is designed to setup an interest in the chapter while acting as an introduction.

PREVIEW
This section is designed to help you think through the purpose of what you want to learn before you actually learn it.

FEATURE PRESENTATION
Each day features a scripture passage on the left that corresponds with the questions on the right. Each question is designed to get you to process God's Word in order to apply it to your life. In the same way, each day's questions are designed to be completed in as little as five minutes. I believe that you need to feel successful in your daily devotions, and by minimizing the time required, you will build a foundation for deeper Spiritual growth.

CREDITS
This section is designed to be used as the application to the study you will have done over the course of the week.

RECAP YOUR THOUGHTS
These journals are designed for you to begin to practice the discipline of recording what God is teaching you in your personal walk with Christ.

TALK TO GOD
This part of the book is designed for you to write out your prayer requests.

Introduction

MEMORY VERSE

By focusing on one verse weekly, you will begin putting into practice what you are studying and memorizing. I feel it is extremely important for you to begin to live your faith out rather than strictly filling yourself with knowledge.

My prayer is that God will totally rock your life in a way that causes you to step up and step out for Jesus on your campus. I believe that Junior High students, like yourself, can make a difference in this world. However, you must be willing for God to use you. Don't be afraid to grow in your walk with Christ, because it is the number one coolest thing you can ever do in life. God wants to use you. Let Him.

Jeremy Tullis
President JuniorHigh4u.com
Fresno, California

In today's I don't care society, your student needs A Fully-Loaded Life: Spiritual Fruit devotional. As a believer, your student's goal in life should be to glorify God with their heart, soul, mind, and actions. Having been in Jr. High ministry for 3 years, I have not seen any other youth devotion available to fully equip students in the same manner.

Pastor Jeremy Tullis brings God to life in this devotional and helps the learner understand God's relevance to his or her life in the 21st century. Your student will understand what it is to be fully-loaded for Christ—that is to live, grow, and flourish through the implementation of the Fruit of the Spirit. He or she will grow in Christ through diligent devotional practices encouraged by this book.

This devotional series is essential for the youth of today because it provides the depth necessary for spiritual growth. The easy-to-understand format helps students feel the success of accomplishment in their devotional life. Success is fostered by minimizing the required time asked of them each day, while still providing the fundamental doctrines of God's Word.

With the Internet, television, and radio, wrong signals are being sent daily to our students. These signals are hate, anger, strife, hostility, impatience, lust, malice, self-indulgence, and many others that will destroy their lives and tear them away from God. By developing a fully-loaded life, today's students will be able to discern between God's ways, which lead to life, and worldly ways, which lead to death.

The attention-grabbing writing style helps to engage students in a life-changing thirst for God. My firsthand experience has proven this to be true. The lives of seven Jr. High boys dramatically changed after completing this first volume of the Fully-Loaded Life series. They became less focused on themselves and more focused on God and each other. They grew in the Spirit, and years later have continued in their desire to spend time with Him daily.

Written for individuals and small groups alike, this Fully-Loaded Life devotional series has, is, and will continue to grow each student, volunteer, and ministry into a deeper unity with Christ. When put into full use, no life will be the same. If you want your youth ministry or student to grow closer to Christ, this devotional will equip them for that purpose. God is close to those who seek Him, so help your student seek Him with all their heart.

Dustin Heiner
Volunteer Staff

The Lost Son

weekly verse

Luke 15:32
"But we had to celebrate and be
glad, because this brother of yours
was dead and is alive again; he was
lost and is found."

A Fully-Loaded Life

TRAILER

Picture this: School's out! You and your friends are bored hanging out at your house. If only you had some money. However, since you're under 15 years old, you cannot get a job. A few hours go by, and you become antsy. You walk into your parent's room and just "happen" to find one of their "platinum" credit cards. Now you can have some fun. So you and your friends take a road trip and party hard. You're gone for a week or two. You party too hard, though, and you max the credit card out. Because you're out of money, your friends disown you, you are freezing on the streets, and you're eating out of garbage cans. You feel so guilty and ashamed of what you have done; you know you cannot go home. You also know that if you live on the streets you might die, so you make up your mind to go home. You decide that you will tell your parents that you messed up big time, and you will live in the dog house out back. You know you do not deserve their love and trust. To your surprise, your parents blow your demands off and throw a party in your honor. Instead of being angry with you, they are totally stoked you are home! How would you feel? Why would your parents do such a thing?

This week we are going to look at a story just like this one from the Bible. We will see that the father accepted his son back after messing up big time because of one underlying character trait— "LOVE". For it is only by loving like God loves that one can truly experience God's ultimate love.

***Check out Galatians 5:22 and list
"The Fruit of the Spirit" ***

_____   _____
_____   _____
_____   _____
_____   _____
_____

PREVIEW

- Tell your group of a time this past week when you were faced with a decision to love someone.

First Things First

Beginning with the end in mind helps you think through the purpose of what you want to learn before you actually learn it.

- What was your decision? Did you accept them? Did you make fun of them? Why/Why not?

- Have you ever been shown love at a time you did not deserve it? What did you do?

- Why did that person show you love? How did it make you feel?

FEATURE PRESENTATION
FEATURE PRESENTATION

If we truly desire to follow Jesus then we must act like Jesus. That means we must be willing to forgive others when they offend us. If we forgive, then that's the first step toward showing love. We cannot show love to another person without first forgiving them. The hardest part about striving to be like Jesus is that we are called to "...love our neighbors as ourselves." Let's take a look at a passage in the Bible that deals with this sacrificial love.

A Fully-Loaded Life

Read **Luke 15:11-32**.

- According to this passage, what do you think love looks like?

Jesus continued: "There was a man who had two sons. ¹²The younger one said to his father, 'Father, give me my share of the estate.' So he divided his property between them.

-Luke 15:11-12

- In verse 12, why do you think the younger son wanted his inheritance so early?

- How do you think he made his father feel by asking for his inheritance?

- What are some modern day inheritances that you want now, refuse to wait for, and can totally mess up your life?

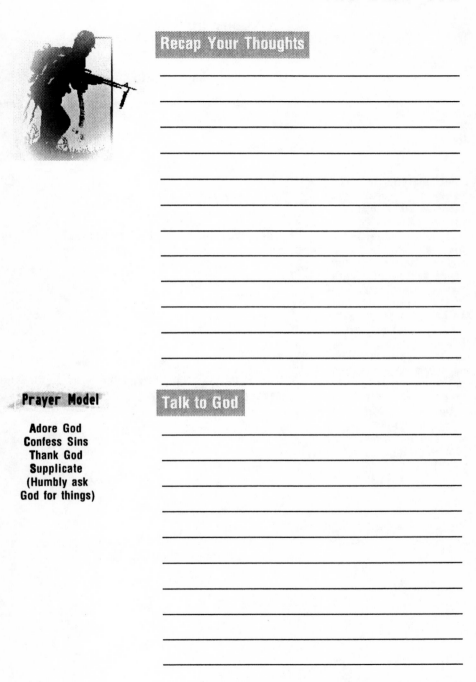

Recap Your Thoughts

_____
_____
_____
_____
_____
_____
_____
_____
_____
_____
_____
_____
_____
_____

Prayer Model

**Adore God
Confess Sins
Thank God
Supplicate
(Humbly ask
God for things)**

Talk to God

_____
_____
_____
_____
_____
_____
_____
_____
_____
_____
_____
_____
_____

A Fully-Loaded Life

Check Out **Luke 15:13-16.**

- What happened once he received his inheritance?

"Not long after that, the younger son got together all he had, set off for a distant country and there squandered his wealth in wild living. ¹⁴After he had spent everything, there was a severe famine in that whole country, and he began to be in need. ¹⁵So he went and hired himself out to a citizen of that country, who sent him to his fields to feed pigs. ¹⁶He longed to fill his stomach with the pods that the pigs were eating, but no one gave him anything.

-Luke 15:13-16

- Why was this young man so foolish?

- What is one way you can throw away blessings that people give you?

- In your opinion, does this young man deserve a second chance? Why/why not?

Recap Your Thoughts

_____
_____
_____
_____
_____
_____
_____
_____
_____
_____
_____
_____

Prayer

This is your chance to document the workings of God in your life.

Talk to God

_____
_____
_____
_____
_____
_____
_____
_____
_____
_____

A Fully-Loaded Life

When he came to his senses, he said, 'How many of my father's hired men have food to spare, and here I am starving to death! ¹⁸I will set out and go back to my father and say to him: Father, I have sinned against heaven and against you. ¹⁹I am no longer worthy to be called your son; make me like one of your hired men.' ²⁰So he got up and went to his father. But while he was still a long way off, his father saw him and was filled with compassion for him; he ran to his son, threw his arms around him and kissed him. ²¹"The son said to him, 'Father, I have sinned against heaven and against you. I am no longer worthy to be called your son.' ²²But the father said to his servants, 'Quick! Bring the best robe and put it on him. Put a ring on his finger and sandals on his feet. ²³Bring the fattened calf and kill it. Let's have a feast and celebrate. ²⁴For this son of mine was dead and is alive again; he was lost and is found.' So they began to celebrate.

-Luke 15:17-24

Check Out **Luke 15:17-24**.

- What did the young man decide to do?

- Why was this so difficult for him?

- What happened when his father saw him?

- Do you think it was easy for his father to love him again? Why/why not?

- What does Jesus mean in verse 24, "For this son of mine was dead and has now returned to life...?"

Recap Your Thoughts

_____
_____
_____
_____
_____
_____
_____
_____
_____
_____
_____
_____

Prayer

The extreme thing about prayer is that God listens.

Talk to God

_____
_____
_____
_____
_____
_____
_____
_____
_____
_____

A Fully-Loaded Life

Check Out Luke 15:25-32.

"Meanwhile, the older son was in the field. When he came near the house, he heard music and dancing. ²⁶So he called one of the servants and asked him what was going on. ²⁷ 'Your brother has come,' he replied, 'and your father has killed the fattened calf because he has him back safe and sound.' ²⁸"The older brother became angry and refused to go in. So his father went out and pleaded with him. ²⁹But he answered his father, 'Look! All these years I've been slaving for you and never disobeyed your orders. Yet you never gave me even a young goat so I could celebrate with my friends. ³⁰But when this son of yours who has squandered your property with prostitutes comes home, you kill the fattened calf for him!' ³¹ 'My son,' the father said, 'you are always with me, and everything I have is yours. ³²But we had to celebrate and be glad, because this brother of yours was dead and is alive again; he was lost and is found.'"

-Luke 15:25-32

- Why was his older brother upset?

- Why did the older son refuse to forgive his brother?

- Why was the father so quick to forgive his son?

- Are you like the older brother? Meaning, do you find yourself judging those "huge" sinners who accept Jesus into their hearts? Do you question their decision instead of praising God for pulling them out of the depths of hell?

- What is the underlying theme of this story told by Jesus?

The Lost Son

Recap Your Thoughts

_____
_____
_____
_____
_____
_____
_____
_____
_____
_____
_____
_____
_____
_____

Why Pray?

Prayer is the action of engaging your heart with the heart of God.

Talk to God

_____
_____
_____
_____
_____
_____
_____
_____
_____
_____
_____
_____

A Fully-Loaded Life

CREDITS

1. How was the father's love sacrificial?

2. Evaluate your life. Is there an area that you need to turn over to God so you can begin to love others?

The credits section is designed to help you apply this week's chapter to your life. It can also be used for further discussion in a small group setting.

3. In this story who does the father represent?

4. Would your friends say you are more like the older brother, younger brother, or the father? Why?

Sacrificial love means loving a person when it costs you everything. God gave his son Jesus to die on the cross. Are you able to give up your pride and popularity in order to forgive those students that upset you daily? Are you able to show Jesus to them?

Recap Your Thoughts

_____
_____
_____
_____
_____
_____
_____
_____
_____
_____
_____
_____
_____
_____

Why Pray?

A fully-loaded life centers on the reality that prayer works.

Talk to God

_____
_____
_____
_____
_____
_____
_____
_____
_____
_____
_____
_____

A Fully-Loaded Life

MEMORY VERSE

"But we had to celebrate and be glad, because this brother of yours was dead and is alive again; he was lost and is found.'"

- Luke 15:32

Living It Out

As a Junior High student, it is time to begin to live your faith out rather than strictly filling yourself up with knowledge. By focusing on one verse weekly, you're given the chance to put into practice what you have been studying. It's up to you to live it out!

How can I apply this lesson to my life?

How can I apply this lesson at school?

Recap Your Thoughts

_____

_____

_____

_____

_____

_____

_____

_____

_____

_____

_____

_____

Why Pray?

God moves in
big ways when
students pray.

Talk to God

_____

_____

_____

_____

_____

_____

_____

_____

_____

_____

_____

_____

A Fully-Loaded Life

REWIND

1. What has God promised me this week?

Keeping It Real

When he came to his senses, he said, 'How many of my father's hired men have food to spare, and here I am starving to death! [18]I will set out and go back to my father and say to him: Father, I have sinned against heaven and against you. [19]I am no longer worthy to be called your son; make me like one of your hired men.' [20]So he got up and went to his father... [24]For this son of mine was dead and is alive again; he was lost and is found.' So they began to celebrate.

-Luke 15:17-24

2. Does God have anything for me to obey?

3. Have I done anything that I need forgiveness from God for?

4. What lesson does God want me to remember this week?

Things I do not understand about this chapter...

_____

_____

_____

_____

_____

_____

Recap Your Thoughts

_____
_____
_____
_____
_____
_____
_____
_____
_____
_____
_____
_____
_____
_____
_____

Just Pray

Prayer is your channel to dialogue with God whenever and wherever you'd like.

Talk to God

_____
_____
_____
_____
_____
_____
_____
_____
_____
_____
_____

The Lost Sheep

weekly verse

Luke 15:10

"In the same way, I tell you, there is rejoicing in the presence of the angels of God over one sinner who repents."

A Fully-Loaded Life

TRAILER

Imagine this: For your birthday all you want is one hundred exotic fish. You love fish. You have been begging your mom, dad, grandparents, aunts, uncles, and friends for months. Your big day is finally here; the moment of truth has arrived. Did you get the fish you wanted? YES! You got all of them, and you are so excited. These are some of the rarest fish in the world. As you go up to your room and begin dumping them into your fish tank, you count each one to find there are ninety-nine in the tank. You begin to panic because you have lost one. You leave the ninety-nine in the tank knowing they will be safe and begin searching for the lost one. You're scared because you know that your neighbor's cat has been lurking on the window sill of your house watching your every move. The race is on. You must find the fish before the cat does. You race through each and every room of your house, flipping over furniture, throwing couch cushions off, ripping off the dry wall. You are truly desperate. Finally, you have an awesome idea. You back track the steps you took to your room. In doing so, you find the fish hanging from the chandelier in the hallway. He must have flown up there when you gave Uncle Buford a high five on your way up the stairs. Anyway, you call all your party guests to the living room to alert them that everything is fine and that you have found "Mr. Fish." Everybody is so happy. They bust out the trumpets and kazoos and all is merry on your birthday.

This week we are going to check out a story from the Bible that is similar to this. The difference is Jesus uses sheep and coins to illustrate His point, not fish. We will discover that "pure joy and peace" comes not from being cool or doing whatever your friends approve as popular. No! It's knowing Jesus and telling others about Him.

PREVIEW

- Were you filled with joy this past week? Why/why not?

First Things First

Beginning with the end in mind helps you think through the purpose of what you want to learn before you actually learn it.

- Tell your group members one way you were able to bring joy to somebody's life over the past week.

- Were you filled with peace this past week? Why/why not?

- Tell your group members one thing that caused you not to have peace in your life this past week.

FEATURE PRESENTATION

When I think of joy I think of Christmas. Christmas is probably the most joyful time of year for me, because no matter what happens in my life, my heart and mind are constantly pulled back to the thought of Jesus being born. The words, "joyful, joyful, we adore Thee," communicate a desperate longing to adore God. However, in order for me to adore God, I must come with a joyful heart, mind, and soul. As you look at a story in the Bible of heaven rejoicing and being filled with joy, think to yourself what it is that God rejoices over. What must you do to get heaven and the angels totally partying?

A Fully-Loaded Life

Read **Luke 15:1-10**.

- According to this passage, what gets heaven rockin' out?

¹Now the tax collectors and "sinners" were all gathering around to hear him. ²But the Pharisees and the teachers of the law muttered, "This man welcomes sinners and eats with them."

-Luke 15:1-2

- What was a Pharisee?

- Why did it bother the Pharisees so much that Jesus hung out with the sinners?

- Do you sometimes act like a "Pharisee" at school with the kids that are "really bad?"

The Lost Sheep

Recap Your Thoughts

_____
_____
_____
_____
_____
_____
_____
_____
_____
_____
_____
_____
_____
_____

Fully Loaded

Acquiring God's presence in your life daily is the first step towards achieving a fully loaded life.

Talk to God

_____
_____
_____
_____
_____
_____
_____
_____
_____
_____
_____

A Fully-Loaded Life

Check Out **Luke 15:3-6**.

- Why does Jesus use the example of "sheep?" What is He referring to?

Then Jesus told them this parable: ⁴"Suppose one of you has a hundred sheep and loses one of them. Does he not leave the ninety-nine in the open country and go after the lost sheep until he finds it? ⁵And when he finds it, he joyfully puts it on his shoulders ⁶and goes home. Then he calls his friends and neighbors together and says, 'Rejoice with me; I have found my lost sheep.'"

-Luke 15:3-6

- Why do you think the shepherd would leave ninety-nine sheep by themselves and go in search for one measly little lamb?

- What is the significance of the man finding the one sheep? How can you relate this passage to your non-Christian friends?

- Why do you think this man was totally joyful when he found his sheep? Why did he call his friends?

_____
_____
_____
_____
_____
_____
_____
_____
_____
_____
_____
_____
_____
_____
_____
_____
_____

Extreme Joy

God wants each of us to do everything joyfully, without complaining, as if we were doing it for Him directly.

Talk to God

_____
_____
_____
_____
_____
_____
_____
_____
_____
_____
_____
_____
_____

A Fully-Loaded Life

Check Out **Luke 15:7**.

- When does heaven rejoice?

> I tell you that in the same way there will be more rejoicing in heaven over one sinner who repents than over ninety-nine righteous persons who do not need to repent.
>
> -Luke 15:7

- Will heaven be throwing a rockin' party for your friends?

- Do you believe that Jesus has sought you out of ninety-nine other people? How does that make you feel?

- What does God seeking us out have to do with us being filled with joy?

Recap Your Thoughts

_____
_____
_____
_____
_____
_____
_____
_____
_____
_____
_____
_____
_____

Prayer

We all should pray in such a way that we demonstrate an authentic humility before God.

Talk to God

_____
_____
_____
_____
_____
_____
_____
_____
_____
_____

A Fully-Loaded Life

Check Out Luke 15:8-10.

- What do you think was so important about the coins?

"Or suppose a woman has ten silver coins and loses one. Does she not light a lamp, sweep the house and search carefully until she finds it? ⁹And when she finds it, she calls her friends and neighbors together and says, 'Rejoice with me; I have found my lost coin.' ¹⁰In the same way, I tell you, there is rejoicing in the presence of the angels of God over one sinner who repents."

-Luke 15:8-10

- Is the woman like the shepherd? How?

- How can you apply these two stories to your life?

- What can you do to stay joyful as you go through today? What can you do to be more like Jesus?

Recap Your Thoughts

_____
_____
_____
_____
_____
_____
_____
_____
_____
_____
_____
_____
_____

Prayer Model

Adoration, Confession, Thanksgiving, and Supplication are four aspects of prayer that each of us must practice in order to live a fully-loaded life for Christ.

Talk to God

_____
_____
_____
_____
_____
_____
_____
_____
_____
_____
_____
_____

A Fully-Loaded Life

CREDITS

1. Evaluate your life. Do you think of yourself as a Pharisee? Do your friends see you as one?

2. How do you demonstrate God's love to your friends and even to strangers?

The credits section is designed to help you apply this week's chapter to your life. It can also be used for further discussion in a small group setting.

3. What makes it hard for you to stay joyful?

4. How can you commit to showing Jesus to your friends? How can you commit to staying joyful?

Pure joy means focusing on Jesus. If you want to experience joy in your life, you must look to Jesus and focus on worshiping Him. By doing this, you will live out Jesus to your friends and indirectly be like the shepherd searching for that one lost sheep. Heaven will rejoice for every soul found. Let's give heaven something to party about. What do you say? Are you with me?

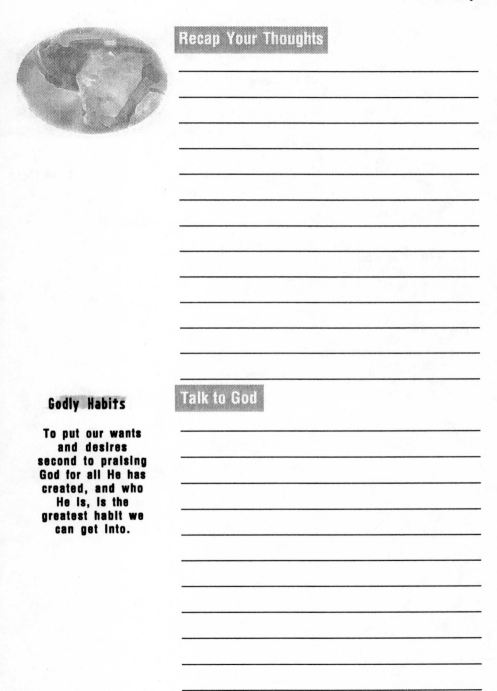

Recap Your Thoughts

Godly Habits

To put our wants and desires second to praising God for all He has created, and who He is, is the greatest habit we can get into.

Talk to God

A Fully-Loaded Life

MEMORY VERSE

In the same way, I tell you, there is rejoicing in the presence of the angels of God over one sinner who repents."

- Luke 15:10

Living It Out

As a Junior High student, it is time to begin to live your faith out rather than strictly filling yourself up with knowledge. By focusing on one verse weekly, you're given the chance to put into practice what you have been studying. It's up to you to live it out!

How can I apply this lesson to my life?

How can I apply this lesson at school?

Recap Your Thoughts

_____
_____
_____
_____
_____
_____
_____
_____
_____
_____
_____
_____
_____

Attitude Check

Our attitudes are the one thing we always have the ability to control.

Talk to God

_____
_____
_____
_____
_____
_____
_____
_____
_____
_____
_____
_____

A Fully-Loaded Life

REWIND

1. What has God promised me this week?

Keeping It Real

I tell you that in the same way there will be more rejoicing in heaven over one sinner who repents than over ninety-nine righteous persons who do not need to repent.

-Luke 15:7

2. Does God have anything for me to obey?

3. Have I done anything that I need forgiveness from God for?

4. What lesson does God want me to remember this week?

Things I do not understand about this chapter...

_____

_____

_____

_____

_____

_____

Recap Your Thoughts

_____
_____
_____
_____
_____
_____
_____
_____
_____
_____
_____
_____
_____
_____

God Listens

God is willing to listen to us; however, we must understand and believe that God's will may be different from our own.

Talk to God

_____
_____
_____
_____
_____
_____
_____
_____
_____
_____
_____
_____

The Hungry Crowd

weekly verse

John 6:14
After the people saw the miraculous sign that Jesus did, they began to say, "Surely this is the Prophet who is to come into the world."

A Fully-Loaded Life

TRAILER

I don't know about you, but my favorite time of day is lunch. I live for lunch. When I was in school I loved opening my lunch bag to see the surprises my mom would put inside for me (this lasted through the twelfth grade). Since my mom always packed my lunch, I knew two things. First, that there was definitely going to be something like gogurt inside, which I love. Second, my sandwich would most likely be smothered with mayo, which I hate. Nonetheless, I always looked forward to lunch. Many days I was so impatient for fifth period to come that I would eat my entire lunch during third period, therefore I had nothing to eat at lunch time. My impatience made me suffer many days at school as I was forced to go without eating for extended intervals. If only I had the patience to wait. If only I had the diligence and perseverance not to fold when my tummy was growling for nourishment. Maybe then I could have left school on a full stomach rather than a starving garbage disposal.

This week we are going to look at a very familiar story in the Bible. We are studying Jesus feeding five-thousand people with only a few loaves of bread and two fish. What will make this story interesting is that we are going to look at the disciples and the crowd this time instead of the little boy. I just wonder if God blessed them because of their patience and diligence to stay and listen to His Son Jesus even when they were hungry.

***Check out Galatians 5:22 and list
"The Fruit of the Spirit" ***

_____   _____
_____   _____
_____   _____
_____   _____
            _____

The Hungry Crowd

PREVIEW

- Think of this past week. Was there a time that you became impatient? Why did you become impatient?

First Things First

Beginning with the end in mind helps you think through the purpose of what you want to learn before you actually learn it.

- What was the consequence of your impatience?

- Now think of a time this past week when you had patience. How did it make you feel? What happened?

- Did God bless you for being patient? Think hard; a blessing comes in many ways. A blessing is something God gives you that you were not expecting. Did you receive a blessing this past week?

FEATURE PRESENTATION

Who is Jabez?

Check out 1 Chronicles 4:9-10.

God wants to extend His blessings to us. Just like Jabez in the Bible, we must ask God daily to extend His blessing and to bless us indeed! However, I believe that God tests us daily by placing obstacles in our way that could cause us to get upset. It might be traffic going too slowly, somebody at McDonald's taking 30 minutes to get your quarter pounder meal, or it might just be someone sitting next to you in class bugging you. Nevertheless, you have a choice. The choice is, "Will you be patient, or will you get upset?"

As you look at this story, think to yourself what the people in the crowd must have been feeling. Think to yourself what the disciples must have been feeling. Did God bless them with food because they were diligent in seeking after Him regardless of how hungry they were? Are you patient enough to wait for God's blessings?

A Fully-Loaded Life

When Jesus heard what had happened, he withdrew by boat privately to a solitary place. Hearing of this, the crowds followed him on foot from the towns. ¹⁴When Jesus landed and saw a large crowd, he had compassion on them and healed their sick.
¹⁵As evening approached, the disciples came to him and said, "This is a remote place, and it's already getting late. Send the crowds away, so they can go to the villages and buy themselves some food." ¹⁶Jesus replied, "They do not need to go away. You give them something to eat."
¹⁷"We have here only five loaves of bread and two fish," they answered. ¹⁸"Bring them here to me," he said. ¹⁹And he directed the people to sit down on the grass. Taking the five loaves and the two fish and looking up to heaven, he gave thanks and broke the loaves. Then he gave them to the disciples, and the disciples gave them to the people. ²⁰They all ate and were satisfied, and the disciples picked up twelve basketfuls of broken pieces that were left over. ²¹The number of those who ate was about five thousand men, besides women and children.

-Matthew 14:13-21

Day One

Read **Matthew 14:13-21**.

- What stands out to you in this passage?

- In verse 15, do you think that the disciples were becoming impatient with the crowd? Why or why not?

Recap Your Thoughts

_____
_____
_____
_____
_____
_____
_____
_____
_____
_____
_____
_____
_____

Why Pray?

When we pray to God, we are communicating with the most powerful being ever.

- Dustin Heiner

Talk to God

_____
_____
_____
_____
_____
_____
_____
_____
_____
_____
_____
_____

A Fully-Loaded Life

The apostles gathered around Jesus and reported to him all they had done and taught. ³¹Then, because so many people were coming and going that they did not even have a chance to eat, he said to them, "Come with me by yourselves to a quiet place and get some rest." ³²So they went away by themselves in a boat to a solitary place. ³³But many who saw them leaving recognized them and ran on foot from all the towns and got there ahead of them. ³⁴When Jesus landed and saw a large crowd, he had compassion on them, because they were like sheep without a shepherd. So he began teaching them many things. ³⁵By this time it was late in the day, so his disciples came to him. "This is a remote place," they said, "and it's already very late. ³⁶Send the people away so they can go to the surrounding countryside and villages and buy themselves something to eat." ³⁷But he answered, "You give them something to eat." They said to him, "That would take eight months of a man's wages! Are we to go and spend that much on bread and give it to them to eat?" ³⁸"How many loaves do you have?" he asked. "Go and see." When they found out, they said, "Five—and two fish." ³⁹Then Jesus directed them to have all the people sit down in groups on the green grass. ⁴⁰So they sat down in groups of hundreds and fifties. ⁴¹Taking the five loaves and the two fish and looking up to heaven, he gave thanks and broke the loaves. Then he gave them to his disciples to set before the people. He also divided the two fish among them all. ⁴²They all ate and were satisfied, ⁴³and the disciples picked up twelve basketfuls of broken pieces of bread and fish. ⁴⁴The number of the men who had eaten was five thousand.

-Mark 6:30-44

Day Two

Check out **Mark 6:30-44.**

- Why do you think Jesus hung-out with the crowd even though He was tired and worn out? What was His main purpose?

- What was Jesus' response to the disciple's impatience?

- How did the disciples react to Jesus?

- Do you think the disciples really wanted to care for the crowd's hunger? Why or why not? Did the disciples care more about their hunger or everyone else's?

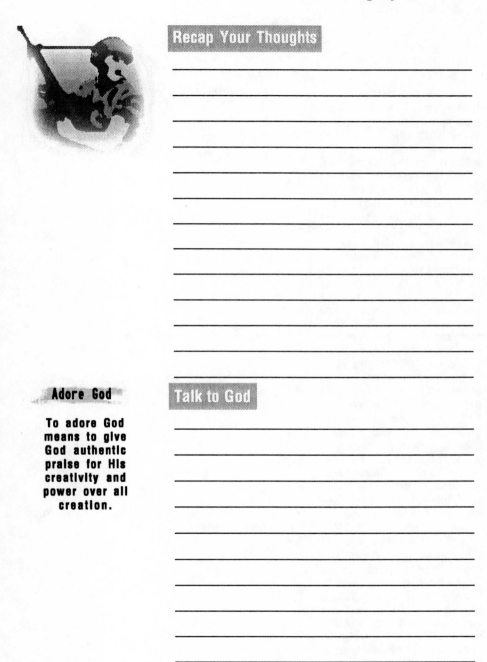

Recap Your Thoughts

_____

_____

_____

_____

_____

_____

_____

_____

_____

_____

_____

_____

_____

Adore God

To adore God means to give God authentic praise for His creativity and power over all creation.

Talk to God

_____

_____

_____

_____

_____

_____

_____

_____

_____

_____

_____

A Fully-Loaded Life

Read **Luke 9:10-17**.

When the apostles returned, they reported to Jesus what they had done. Then he took them with him and they withdrew by themselves to a town called Bethsaida, [11]but the crowds learned about it and followed him. He welcomed them and spoke to them about the kingdom of God, and healed those who needed healing. [12]Late in the afternoon the Twelve came to him and said, "Send the crowd away so they can go to the surrounding villages and countryside and find food and lodging, because we are in a remote place here." [13]He replied, "You give them something to eat." [14]They answered, "We have only five loaves of bread and two fish—unless we go and buy food for all this crowd." (About five thousand men were there.) [15]But he said to his disciples, "Have them sit down in groups of about fifty each." The disciples did so, and everybody sat down. [16]Taking the five loaves and the two fish and looking up to heaven, he gave thanks and broke them. Then he gave them to the disciples to set before the people. [17]They all ate and were satisfied, and the disciples picked up twelve basketfuls of broken pieces that were left over.

-Luke 9:10-17

*Did you know that the 5000 people only included men? There were also women and children present that were not counted.

- What happened when Jesus was given the five loaves of bread and two fish?

- Why did the crowd follow Jesus?

- How do you think the crowd of 5000+ was reacting to their hunger?

The Hungry Crowd

_____
_____
_____
_____
_____
_____
_____
_____
_____
_____
_____
_____
_____
_____

Prayer Warrior

It takes a person with an extremely Godly character to live a life of authentic prayer.

Talk to God

_____
_____
_____
_____
_____
_____
_____
_____
_____
_____
_____
_____
_____

A Fully-Loaded Life

Some time after this, Jesus crossed to the far shore of the Sea of Galilee (that is, the Sea of Tiberias), ²and a great crowd of people followed him because they saw the miraculous signs he had performed on the sick. ³Then Jesus went up on a mountainside and sat down with his disciples. ⁴The Jewish Passover Feast was near. ⁵When Jesus looked up and saw a great crowd coming toward him, he said to Philip, "Where shall we buy bread for these people to eat?" ⁶He asked this only to test him, for he already had in mind what he was going to do. ⁷Philip answered him, "Eight months' wages would not buy enough bread for each one to have a bite!" ⁸Another of his disciples, Andrew, Simon Peter's brother, spoke up, ⁹"Here is a boy with five small barley loaves and two small fish, but how far will they go among so many?" ¹⁰Jesus said, "Have the people sit down." There was plenty of grass in that place, and the men sat down, about five thousand of them. ¹¹Jesus then took the loaves, gave thanks, and distributed to those who were seated as much as they wanted. He did the same with the fish. ¹²When they had all had enough to eat, he said to his disciples, "Gather the pieces that are left over. Let nothing be wasted." ¹³So they gathered them and filled twelve baskets with the pieces of the five barley loaves left over by those who had eaten. ¹⁴After the people saw the miraculous sign that Jesus did, they began to say, "Surely this is the Prophet who is to come into the world." ¹⁵Jesus, knowing that they intended to come and make him king by force, withdrew again to a mountain by himself.

-John 6:1-15

Day Four

Check out **John 6:1-15**.

- When the disciples began passing out the bread and fish what happened?

- What does verse 14 mean?

- How would you have felt being a disciple-- hungry, tired, and hot and now you have to pass out the food to all 5000+ people?

- Do you think Jesus was working on His disciple's patience forcing them to eat last?

Recap Your Thoughts

_____

_____

_____

_____

_____

_____

_____

_____

_____

_____

_____

My Direct Line

Prayer is the
line we connect
to in order for
God to give us
that extra touch
of love.

Talk to God

_____

_____

_____

_____

_____

_____

_____

_____

_____

_____

A Fully-Loaded Life

CREDITS

1. What makes a person impatient?

2. Why was the crowd of thousands so patient to receive their food?

The credits section is designed to help you apply this week's chapter to your life. It can also be used for further discussion in a small group setting.

3. Why were the disciples so impatient?

4. How are you going to be more patient this week? Write down 3 ways:
   a)

   b)

   c)

Patience comes from your heart. If you are impatient with others it is probably because you are only thinking of yourself. The disciples wanted the crowd to leave and go home, maybe just so they could eat, but probably they were tired too. They were thinking only of themselves. The crowd was patient probably because they were waiting to see Jesus perform a miracle. Jesus is waiting for us to slow down and focus on our friends instead of ourselves. Only then will we truly experience the awesomeness of God.

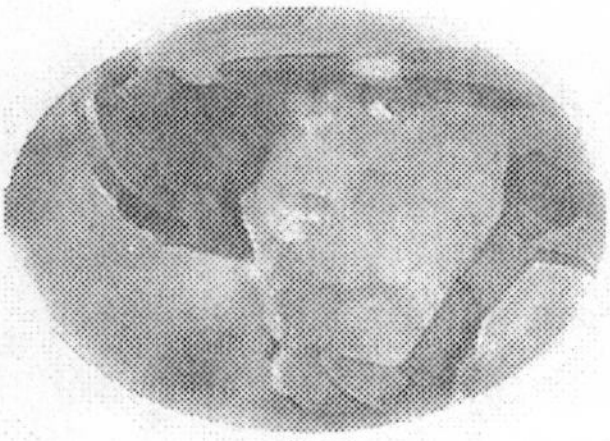

The Hungry Crowd

Recap Your Thoughts

_____
_____
_____
_____
_____
_____
_____
_____
_____
_____
_____
_____
_____

Got Jesus?

God wants
one thing
from you...
your life.

Talk to God

_____
_____
_____
_____
_____
_____
_____
_____
_____
_____
_____
_____

A Fully-Loaded Life

MEMORY VERSE

After the people saw the miraculous sign that Jesus did, they began to say, "Surely this is the Prophet who is to come into the world."

- John 6:14

Living It Out

As a Junior High student, it is time to begin to live your faith out rather than strictly filling yourself up with knowledge. By focusing on one verse weekly, you're given the chance to put into practice what you have been studying. It's up to you to live it out!

How can I apply this lesson to my life?

How can I apply this lesson at school?

Recap Your Thoughts

_____

_____

_____

_____

_____

_____

_____

_____

_____

_____

_____

_____

_____

Fully-Loaded

A fully-loaded ifle centers on the reality that prayer works.

Talk to God

_____

_____

_____

_____

_____

_____

_____

_____

_____

_____

_____

A Fully-Loaded Life

REWIND

1. What has God promised me this week?

Keeping It Real

When Jesus heard what had happened, he withdrew by boat privately to a solitary place. Hearing of this, the crowds followed him on foot from the towns. ¹⁴When Jesus landed and saw a large crowd, he had compassion on them and healed their sick. ¹⁵As evening approached, the disciples came to him and said, "This is a remote place, and it's already getting late. Send the crowds away, so they can go to the villages and buy themselves some food." ¹⁶Jesus replied, "They do not need to go away. You give them something to eat...."

-Matthew 14:12-21

2. Does God have anything for me to obey?

3. Have I done anything that I need forgiveness from God for?

4. What lesson does God want me to remember this week?

Things I do not understand about this chapter...

_____

_____

_____

_____

_____

_____

The Hungry Crowd

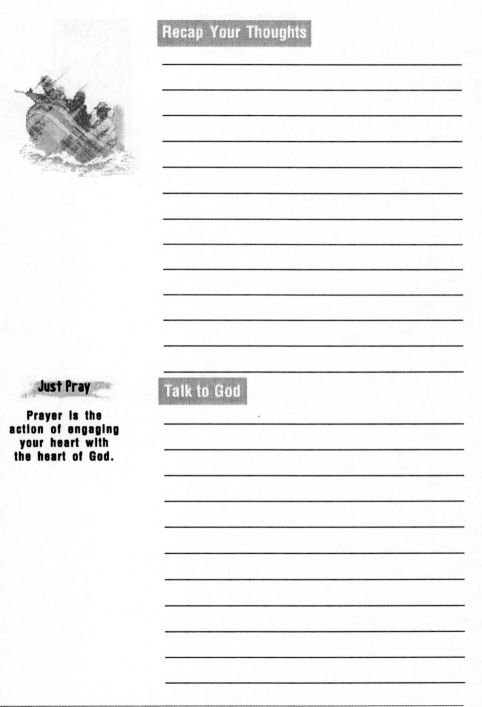

Recap Your Thoughts

_____
_____
_____
_____
_____
_____
_____
_____
_____
_____
_____
_____

Just Pray

Prayer is the
action of engaging
your heart with
the heart of God.

Talk to God

_____
_____
_____
_____
_____
_____
_____
_____
_____
_____
_____

The Kind Man

weekly verse

Luke 10:27

..."'Love the Lord your God with all your heart and with all your soul and with all your strength and with all your mind'; and, 'Love your neighbor as yourself.'"

A Fully-Loaded Life

Have you ever been picked on at school? Have you ever been bullied around? How does it make you feel? Imagine that you were at school and a group of punks jumped you behind the lockers. They beat you down to the ground. They sole your wallet with your lunch money in it, dumped soda all over you, and even spit in your face. You were so embarrassed and hurt that you couldn't even help yourself up. Finally, your vice-principal walked by on the way back to her office and looked at you lying on the ground. You motion and grunt for help, but she didn't want to get her dress messy. So, she turned around and walked to her office the back way. Later, your fourth period math teacher passed by. You hadn't performed so well in his class, however, so he opted not to help you either. You gave up! Nobody would help you in your darkest moment of need.

An hour went by, finally a geek with capri pants walked up and asks if he could help you. You were totally surprised because this was the same kid you made fun of a week ago for smelling like your grandmother's armpit. Things just didn't add up. No one at your school likes this guy, yet when one of the very people that made fun of him was hurt, he was kind enough to stop and help. As this geek helped you up, you felt pretty stupid because of the way you had treated him. Soon you and he become the best of friends.

This week we are going to look at a story, much like this one, which deals with extreme kindness. So grab your Bibles and let's dive in!

***Check out Galatians 5:22 and list
"The Fruit of the Spirit" ***

_____   _____
_____   _____
_____   _____
_____   _____
         _____

64

PREVIEW

- Do you see yourself as a kind person?

First Things First

Beginning with the end in mind helps you think through the purpose of what you want to learn before you actually learn it.

- In this past week, who have you shown kindness to?

- Have you been aware of your actions towards others? If so, how?

FEATURE PRESENTATION

This week we are exploring how God wants us to be kind to others. I know from experience that this is a very difficult task to accomplish. Kindness is possible, however, and very rewarding when practiced regularly. We are going to look at what it is like to be the one who is on the receiving side of kindness. We are going to look at a story about a man who has been beaten and left to die. The only reason he lives is because a man (the last man this cripple would expect to see help him) was kind enough to do just that. We want to learn by the end of our week together how and why we need to be kind to those we do not like and even hate. Right now ask God to open your heart and show you one or two people in your life you need to practice being kind to.

A Fully-Loaded Life

Check out **Luke 10:25-29.**

- In verse 25, what kind of person was it that was asking Jesus this question?

On one occasion an expert in the law stood up to test Jesus. "Teacher," he asked, "what must I do to inherit eternal life?" 26"What is written in the Law?" he replied. "How do you read it?" 27He answered: "'Love the Lord your God with all your heart and with all your soul and with all your strength and with all your mind'; and, 'Love your neighbor as yourself.'" 28"You have answered correctly," Jesus replied. "Do this and you will live." 29But he wanted to justify himself, so he asked Jesus, "And who is my neighbor?"

-Luke 10:25-29

- What law was Jesus referring to?

  HINT: check out Deuteronomy 6:5-6.

- What was this "expert's" answer?

- In your opinion, would this "expert's" answer hold up in a court of law? Why/why not?

- Even though he answered Jesus' question correctly, what was the one problem with his answer (You're going to have to think)?

Recap Your Thoughts

_____

_____

_____

_____

_____

_____

_____

_____

_____

_____

_____

_____

_____

God Listens

In order to live a fully-loaded life, you must have a constant communication with God.

-Dustin Heiner

Talk to God

_____

_____

_____

_____

_____

_____

_____

_____

_____

_____

_____

_____

A Fully-Loaded Life

Read Luke 10:30-31.

- What happened to this innocent man?

In reply Jesus said: "A man was going down from Jerusalem to Jericho, when he fell into the hands of robbers. They stripped him of his clothes, beat him and went away, leaving him half dead. ³¹A priest happened to be going down the same road, and when he saw the man, he passed by on the other side..."

-Luke 10:30-31

- What is the deal with the priest? Write out how you would feel if a priest or pastor did the same thing to you when you were half dead.

- Why do you think the priest avoided this man?

The Kind Man

Recap Your Thoughts

_____
_____
_____
_____
_____
_____
_____
_____
_____
_____
_____
_____
_____
_____

Prayer

This is your chance to document the workings of God in your life.

Talk to God

_____
_____
_____
_____
_____
_____
_____
_____
_____
_____
_____
_____

A Fully-Loaded Life

Take a look at **Luke 10:30-32**.

- What is up with these religious men?

In reply Jesus said: "A man was going down from Jerusalem to Jericho, when he fell into the hands of robbers. They stripped him of his clothes, beat him and went away, leaving him half dead. [31]A priest happened to be going down the same road, and when he saw the man, he passed by on the other side. [32]So too, a Levite, when he came to the place and saw him, passed by on the other side..."

-Luke 10:30-32

- How are your actions similar to those of the religious men?

- Do you try to avoid messy problems? What is it that keeps you from showing those in need kindness?

Recap Your Thoughts

_____
_____
_____
_____
_____
_____
_____
_____
_____
_____
_____
_____
_____
_____

Prayer

The extreme thing about prayer is that God listens.

Talk to God

_____
_____
_____
_____
_____
_____
_____
_____
_____
_____
_____

A Fully-Loaded Life

Check out the end of this story in
Luke 10:33-37.

- Who were the Samaritans?

But a Samaritan, as he traveled, came where the man was; and when he saw him, he took pity on him. ³⁴He went to him and bandaged his wounds, pouring on oil and wine. Then he put the man on his own donkey, took him to an inn and took care of him. ³⁵The next day he took out two silver coins and gave them to the innkeeper. 'Look after him,' he said, 'and when I return, I will reimburse you for any extra expense you may have.' ³⁶"Which of these three do you think was a neighbor to the man who fell into the hands of robbers?" ³⁷The expert in the law replied, "The one who had mercy on him." Jesus told him, "Go and do likewise."

-Luke 10:33-37

- Why did this outcast Samaritan man help a Jewish man?

- What do you think the significance of the Samaritan paying the innkeeper is?

- In this story, who does Jesus say our neighbor is?

Recap Your Thoughts

_____
_____
_____
_____
_____
_____
_____
_____
_____
_____
_____
_____
_____
_____

Why Pray?

Prayer is the action of engaging your heart with the heart of God.

Talk to God

_____
_____
_____
_____
_____
_____
_____
_____
_____
_____
_____

A Fully-Loaded Life

CREDITS

1. After completing this lesson, why is it important to be kind?

The credits section is designed to help you apply this week's chapter to your life. It can also be used for further discussion in a small group setting.

2. How do you think people will view church and Jesus Christ if we are kind to everyone we encounter?

3. What are some practical ways to show kindness to people?

4. List 4 people you are going to be kind to this week.

_____

_____

_____

_____

Recap Your Thoughts

_____

_____

_____

_____

_____

_____

_____

_____

_____

_____

_____

_____

_____

_____

Why Pray?

A fully-loaded life centers on the reality that prayer works.

Talk to God

_____

_____

_____

_____

_____

_____

_____

_____

_____

_____

_____

_____

_____

A Fully-Loaded Life

MEMORY VERSE

…"'Love the Lord your God with all your heart and with all your soul and with all your strength and with all your mind'; and, 'Love your neighbor as yourself.'"

-Luke 10:27

Living It Out

As a Junior High student, it is time to begin to live your faith out rather than strictly filling yourself up with knowledge. By focusing on one verse weekly, you're given the chance to put into practice what you have been studying. It's up to you to live it out!

How can I apply this lesson to my life?

How can I apply this lesson at school?

Recap Your Thoughts

_____
_____
_____
_____
_____
_____
_____
_____
_____
_____
_____
_____
_____
_____
_____

Why Pray?

God moves in big ways when students pray.

Talk to God

_____
_____
_____
_____
_____
_____
_____
_____
_____
_____
_____
_____

A Fully-Loaded Life

REWIND

1. What has God promised me this week?

Keeping It Real

2. Does God have anything for me to obey?

But a Samaritan, as he traveled, came where the man was; and when he saw him, he took pity on him. 34He went to him and bandaged his wounds, pouring on oil and wine. Then he put the man on his own donkey, took him to an inn and took care of him. 35The next day he took out two silver coins and gave them to the innkeeper. 'Look after him,' he said, 'and when I return, I will reimburse you for any extra expense you may have.' 36"Which of these three do you think was a neighbor to the man who fell into the hands of robbers?" 37The expert in the law replied, "The one who had mercy on him." Jesus told him, "Go and do likewise."

-Luke 10:33-37

3. Have I done anything that I need forgiveness from God for?

4. What lesson does God want me to remember this week?

Things I do not understand about this chapter...

_____

_____

_____

_____

_____

_____

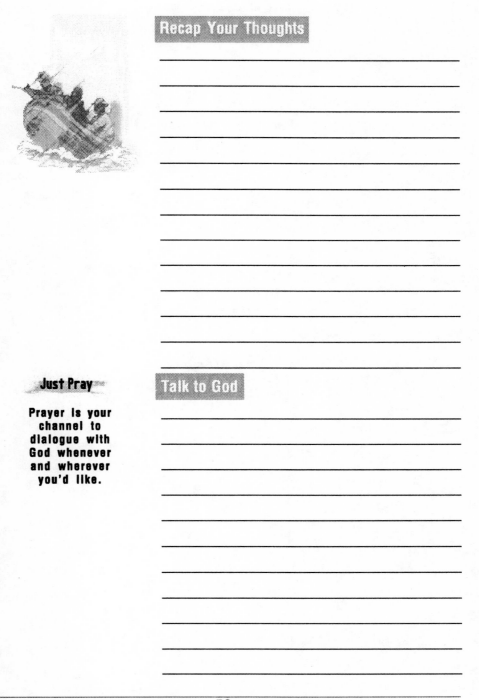

Recap Your Thoughts

_____
_____
_____
_____
_____
_____
_____
_____
_____
_____
_____
_____
_____

Just Pray

Prayer is your channel to dialogue with God whenever and wherever you'd like.

Talk to God

_____
_____
_____
_____
_____
_____
_____
_____
_____
_____
_____
_____

Finding the Good in Another

weekly verse

Matthew 18:26-27

The servant fell on his knees before him. 'Be patient with me,' he begged, 'and I will pay back everything.' [27]The servant's master took pity on him, canceled the debt and let him go.

A Fully-Loaded Life

TRAILER

Everyday I am faced with many decisions concerning the way I am going to react to other human beings. The decisions I make daily directly influence my actions. My actions then directly influence my attitude. If I am striving to be like Jesus in everything I do, I must make difficult decisions that put other people first. Many times I hate doing this. No one likes letting a person cut in front of them at McDonald's to get their food first, or giving up their lunch to a homeless person, however if we are going to be like Jesus, then we must sacrifice.

In this lesson, we are looking at a story in the Bible where one guy forgave another of his debt and by doing so showed him that he really wanted to "do good" towards him. So what are we waiting for? Let's dive in!

***Check out Galatians 5:22 and list
"The Fruit of the Spirit" ***

_____   _____
_____   _____
_____   _____
_____   _____
          _____

Finding the Good in Another

PREVIEW

- Did you do anything good for anyone this week? If so, what was it?

- Do you think that by forgiving people who have wronged you, you would more likley want to do good things for them. Why/Why Not?

- Do you think Jesus ever got sick of doing good things for people? Why/Why Not?

FEATURE PRESENTATION

As you take in God's Word, check out how the one man was to the other who owed him money. As you read this story, think to yourself whether or not you act most like the first person who did good to the one who owed him money, or the second person who began choking the one who owed him money. Ask God to give you a heart of goodness before you begin to plow through this story.

A Fully-Loaded Life

Check out **Matthew 18:21-22.**

- According to this passage, what is so important about forgiving a person four hundred ninety times versus just seven times?

Then Peter came to Jesus and asked, "Lord, how many times shall I forgive my brother when he sins against me? Up to seven times?" [22]Jesus answered, "I tell you, not seven times, but seventy-seven times."

-Matthew 18:21-22

- Why do you think Peter even asked Jesus this question?

- Is it easier to "do good" to another person if we forgive them of wronging us? Why/Why not?

- What is the most difficult part of forgiving somebody?

Recap Your Thoughts

_____
_____
_____
_____
_____
_____
_____
_____
_____
_____
_____
_____
_____
_____
_____

Fully Loaded

Acquiring God's presence in our lives daily is the first step towards achieving a fully loaded life.

Talk to God

_____
_____
_____
_____
_____
_____
_____
_____
_____
_____
_____
_____
_____

A Fully-Loaded Life

Now read **verses 23-26** of **Matthew 18**.

- What is the significance of these verses?

Therefore, the kingdom of heaven is like a king who wanted to settle accounts with his servants. ²⁴As he began the settlement, a man who owed him ten thousand talents was brought to him. ²⁵Since he was not able to pay, the master ordered that he and his wife and his children and all that he had be sold to repay the debt.
²⁶"The servant fell on his knees before him. 'Be patient with me,' he begged, 'and I will pay back everything.'

-Matthew 18:23-26

- What significance is the king? Who do the servants represent?

- What does Jesus mean when He says heaven's like a king who wanted to settle debts?

- How does this passage relate to us today?

Recap Your Thoughts

_____
_____
_____
_____
_____
_____
_____
_____
_____
_____
_____
_____
_____
_____
_____
_____

Extreme Joy

God wants each of us to do everything joyfully, without complaining, as if we were doing it for Him directly.

Talk to God

_____
_____
_____
_____
_____
_____
_____
_____
_____
_____
_____
_____
_____

A Fully-Loaded Life

Then Peter came to Jesus and asked, "Lord, how many times shall I forgive my brother when he sins against me? Up to seven times?" ²²Jesus answered, "I tell you, not seven times, but seventy-seven times. ²³"Therefore, the kingdom of heaven is like a king who wanted to settle accounts with his servants. ²⁴As he began the settlement, a man who owed him ten thousand talents was brought to him. ²⁵Since he was not able to pay, the master ordered that he and his wife and his children and all that he had be sold to repay the debt. ²⁶"The servant fell on his knees before him. 'Be patient with me,' he begged, 'and I will pay back everything.' ²⁷The servant's master took pity on him, canceled the debt and let him go. ²⁸But when that servant went out, he found one of his fellow servants who owed him a hundred denarii. He grabbed him and began to choke him. 'Pay back what you owe me!' he demanded. ²⁹His fellow servant fell to his knees and begged him, 'Be patient with me, and I will pay you back.' ³⁰But he refused. Instead, he went off and had the man thrown into prison until he could pay the debt. ³¹When the other servants saw what had happened, they were greatly distressed and went and told their master everything that had happened.

-Matthew 18:21-31

Check out what happened next in **verses 21-31.**

•   What happened when the king released the servant?

•   In many ways the servant is like you and I isn't he? In what ways are you like the servant?

•   What should the servant have done after being freed of all his debt? What kept him from showing goodness to his own servant?

Finding the Good in Another

_____
_____
_____
_____
_____
_____
_____
_____
_____
_____
_____
_____
_____
_____

Prayer

We all should pray in such a way that we demonstrate an authentic humility before God.

Talk to God

_____
_____
_____
_____
_____
_____
_____
_____
_____
_____
_____
_____
_____

A Fully-Loaded Life

Read the ending from **verses 32-35.**

- What did the king do to the servant he freed from debt?

"Then the master called the servant in. 'You wicked servant,' he said, 'I canceled all that debt of yours because you begged me to. ³³Shouldn't you have had mercy on your fellow servant just as I had on you?' ³⁴In anger his master turned him over to the jailers to be tortured, until he should pay back all he owed. ³⁵This is how my heavenly Father will treat each of you unless you forgive your brother from your heart."

-Matthew 18:32-35

- Why was the king so harsh with him?

- Write out **verse 35.**

- What is the significance of this verse?

- What is the significance of forgiving others?

Finding the Good in Another

_____
_____
_____
_____
_____
_____
_____
_____
_____
_____
_____
_____
_____

Prayer Model

Adoration,
Confession,
Thanksgiving and
Supplication
are four aspects of
prayer that each of
us must practice in
order to live a
fully-loaded life for
Christ.

Talk to God

_____
_____
_____
_____
_____
_____
_____
_____
_____
_____
_____

A Fully-Loaded Life

CREDITS

1. List some ways God has been like the king in the story to you. How has he shown goodness to you?

The credits section is designed to help you apply this week's chapter to your life. It can also be used for further discussion in a small group setting.

2. Who is God telling you to forgive? What are you going to do?

3. Write a plan of attack for this upcoming week and list the ways you are going to begin to forgive others and show goodness to them.

Finding the Good in Another

_____
_____
_____
_____
_____
_____
_____
_____
_____
_____
_____
_____
_____

Godly Habits

To put our wants and desires second to praising God for all He has created, and who He is, is the greatest habit we can get into.

Talk to God

_____
_____
_____
_____
_____
_____
_____
_____
_____
_____
_____

A Fully-Loaded Life

MEMORY VERSE

The servant fell on his knees before him. 'Be patient with me,' he begged, 'and I will pay back everything.' [27]The servant's master took pity on him, canceled the debt and let him go.

- Matthew 18:26-27

Living It Out

As a Junior High student, it is time to begin to live your faith out rather than strictly filling yourself up with knowledge.   By focusing on one verse weekly, you're given the chance to put into practice what you have been studying. It's up to you to live it out!

How can I apply this lesson to my life?

How can I apply this lesson at school?

Finding the Good in Another

Recap Your Thoughts

_____
_____
_____
_____
_____
_____
_____
_____
_____
_____
_____
_____
_____
_____

Attitude Check

Our attitudes are the one thing we always have the ability to control.

Talk to God

_____
_____
_____
_____
_____
_____
_____
_____
_____
_____
_____
_____

A Fully-Loaded Life

REWIND

1. What has God promised me this week?

Keeping It Real

"Then the master called the servant in. 'You wicked servant,' he said, 'I canceled all that debt of yours because you begged me to. ³³Shouldn't you have had mercy on your fellow servant just as I had on you?' ³⁴In anger his master turned him over to the jailers to be tortured, until he should pay back all he owed. ³⁵This is how my heavenly Father will treat each of you unless you forgive your brother from your heart."

-Matthew 18:32-35

2. Does God have anything for me to obey?

3. Have I done anything that I need forgiveness from God for?

4. What lesson does God want me to remember this week?

Things I do not understand about this chapter...

_____

_____

_____

_____

_____

_____

Finding the Good in Another

Recap Your Thoughts

_____

_____

_____

_____

_____

_____

_____

_____

_____

_____

_____

_____

_____

_____

God Listens

God is willing to listen to us; however, we must undertand and believe that God's will may be different from our own.

Talk to God

_____

_____

_____

_____

_____

_____

_____

_____

_____

_____

Show Me the Money

weekly verse

Matthew 25:21

"His master replied, 'Well done, good and faithful servant! You have been faithful with a few things; I will put you in charge of many things. Come and share your master's happiness!'"

TRAILER

Imagine someone giving you one million dollars. What would you do with it? Would you go spend it all on awesome cars like Lamborghinis, Ferraris, or Porsches? Or, would you take a trip to New York and go on an enormous shopping spree buying everything you have ever wanted? Maybe you would invest three-quarters of it in a company like Microsoft and then live on the other one-quarter. Now what if five years later the person who gave you the money came and asked for it back. Well, if you bought cars, clothes, and big mansions you probably wouldn't have any money left. You would have to tell them that you had spent it all. How would that make you feel? Now if you invested most of it into a company like Microsoft, you could look that person in the eye and tell them that you took their one million dollars and turned a profit of one hundred million dollars. How would that make you feel? Would you feel proud of yourself? Do you think that the person with the money would entrust more money to you?

In this lesson we are discussing the importance of faithfulness. We will look at a story similar to this one where three guys are entrusted with money. We will see for ourselves who is faithful and who is not. We will see how God wants us to be faithful with the small things as well as the big things. So let's dive in! What do ya' say?

***Check out Galatians 5:22 and list
"The Fruit of the Spirit" ***

_____   _____
_____   _____
_____   _____
_____   _____

_____

PREVIEW

- Tell your group of a time you were not faithful in following through with something? How did it make you feel? What happened as a consequence of your unfaithfulness?

First Things First

Beginning with the end in mind helps you think through the purpose of what you want to learn before you actually learn it.

- What have you been faithful in this past week? Homework, sports, music, prayer, quiet times, chores, etc.?

- What is one BIG thing that you believe God has entrusted to you to take care of and be faithful with?

FEATURE PRESENTATION

As a follower of Christ, we are called to be faithful. God wants us to be faithful in everything He gives to us. Including friends, money, school, work, sports, etc. If God is going to expand our boundaries (give us bigger and better things), then we must prove to Him that we can handle the small blessings first. Pray that God will open your heart to areas where you are unfaithful. Ask Him to teach you how to be

A Fully-Loaded Life

Read **Matthew 25:14-18.**

"Again, It will be like a man going on a journey, who called his servants and entrusted his property to them. ¹⁵To one he gave five talents of money, to another two talents, and to another one talent, each according to his ability. Then he went on his journey. ¹⁶The man who had received the five talents went at once and put his money to work and gained five more. ¹⁷So also, the one with the two talents gained two more. ¹⁸But the man who had received the one talent went off, dug a hole In the ground and hid his master's money."

-Matthew 25:14-18

- Why do you think the master gave money to his servants?

- Couldn't the master have made just as much, if not more, if he did it himself? Why/why not?

- Write out what the three men did with their money.

- What would you have done with the money? Write out what your plan would have been.

Recap Your Thoughts

_____
_____
_____
_____
_____
_____
_____
_____
_____
_____
_____
_____
_____

Why Pray?

When we pray to God, we are communicating with the most powerful being ever.

- Dustin Heiner

Talk to God

_____
_____
_____
_____
_____
_____
_____
_____
_____
_____
_____

A Fully-Loaded Life

Read **Matthew 25:19-23.**

- What happened in these verses?

"After a long time the master of those servants returned and settled accounts with them. ²⁰The man who had received the five talents brought the other five. 'Master,' he said, 'you entrusted me with five talents. See, I have gained five more.'
²¹"His master replied, 'Well done, good and faithful servant! You have been faithful with a few things; I will put you in charge of many things. Come and share your master's happiness!'" ²²The man with the two talents also came. 'Master,' he said, 'you entrusted me with two talents; see, I have gained two more.'
²³His master replied, 'Well done, good and faithful servant! You have been faithful with a few things; I will put you in charge of many things. Come and share your master's happiness!'

-Matthew 25:19-23

- Were these first two men faithful in what their master left with them? How?

- What happened to these guys when their master found out what they had done with his money?

- If God were to evaluate you, would He say the same thing to you regarding the things He has entrusted you with as this master said to his two servants? Why/why not? What would He say?

Recap Your Thoughts

_____

_____

_____

_____

_____

_____

_____

_____

_____

_____

_____

_____

_____

Adore God

To adore God means to give God authentic praise for His creativity and power over all creation.

Talk to God

_____

_____

_____

_____

_____

_____

_____

_____

_____

_____

_____

A Fully-Loaded Life

Check out **Matthew 25:24-25.**

- What did this servant do with the money that his master gave him?

Then the man who had received the one talent came. "Master," he said, "I knew that you are a hard man, harvesting where you have not sown and gathering where you have not scattered seed. ²⁵So I was afraid and went out and hid your talent in the ground. See, here is what belongs to you."

-Matthew 25:24-25

- Why do you think he did this? Surely he knew what the other two had done with their money, why didn't he do the same?

- How would it make you feel if you entrusted your financial investor with your money and you expected him to be faithful with his investments, but instead of investing it, he buried the money and gave you back the exact same amount that you had given him?

Recap Your Thoughts

_____

_____

_____

_____

_____

_____

_____

_____

_____

_____

_____

_____

_____

Prayer Warrior

It takes a person with an extremely Godly character to live a life of authentic prayer.

Talk to God

_____

_____

_____

_____

_____

_____

_____

_____

_____

_____

_____

_____

A Fully-Loaded Life

Read what happens next in **Matthew 25:26-30.**

- How did the master react to this servant's unfaithfulness?

His master replied, "You wicked, lazy servant! So you knew that I harvest where I have not sown and gather where I have not scattered seed? ²⁷Well then, you should have put my money on deposit with the bankers, so that when I returned I would have received it back with interest. ²⁸ Take the talent from him and give it to the one who has the ten talents. ²⁹For everyone who has will be given more, and he will have an abundance. Whoever does not have, even what he has will be taken from him. ³⁰And throw that worthless servant outside, into the darkness, where there will be weeping and gnashing of teeth."

-Matthew 25:26-30

- Why did the servant choose to hide his master's money in the ground?

- Read verse 29, and re-write it in your own words.

- What is Jesus talking about when He says, "Whoever does not have, even what he has will be taken from him." What is the main point Jesus is getting at?

Recap Your Thoughts

_____

_____

_____

_____

_____

_____

_____

_____

_____

_____

_____

_____

_____

My Direct Line

Prayer is the line we connect to in order for God to give us that extra touch of love.

Talk to God

_____

_____

_____

_____

_____

_____

_____

_____

_____

_____

_____

_____

Day Five

CREDITS

1. From this story, what are some areas you can be faithful in?

2. What are some ways you can show God faithfulness with your money?

The credits section is designed to help you apply this week's chapter to your life. It can also be used for further discussion in a small group setting.

3. Stop right now and ask God where you need to be more faithful. Then, ask Him to show you where to begin putting your thoughts into action.

4. Now list some action steps for yourself on how you can become a person whom God and others can rely on. Start with easy ones and move your way up to harder ones.
   a)
   b)
   c)
   d)

God has called each of us to be faithful in the little things, so he can bless us with more. God is waiting for you to make your mind up: are you going to step up and live for Him? If you accept this challenge and are faithful in being His servant, God will bless you and give you more than you could ever dream of or deserve. What do ya' say? Do you accept His challenge? Are you ready to be faithful?

Recap Your Thoughts

_____
_____
_____
_____
_____
_____
_____
_____
_____
_____
_____
_____
_____
_____
_____

Got Jesus?

**God wants
one thing
from you...
your life.**

Talk to God

_____
_____
_____
_____
_____
_____
_____
_____
_____
_____
_____
_____
_____
_____

A Fully-Loaded Life

MEMORY VERSRE

"His master replied, 'Well done, good and faithful servant! You have been faithful with a few things; I will put you in charge of many things. Come and share your master's happiness!'"

-Matthew 25:21

Living It Out

As a Junior High student, it is time to begin to live your faith out rather than strictly filling yourself up with knowledge. By focusing on one verse weekly, you're given the chance to put into practice what you have been studying. It's up to you to live it out!

How can I apply this lesson to my life?

How can I apply this lesson at school?

Recap Your Thoughts

_____
_____
_____
_____
_____
_____
_____
_____
_____
_____
_____
_____
_____
_____

Fully-Loaded

A fully-loaded life centers on the reality that prayer works.

Talk to God

_____
_____
_____
_____
_____
_____
_____
_____
_____
_____
_____

A Fully-Loaded Life

REWIND

1. What has God promised me this week?

Keeping It Real

"Again, it will be like a man going on a journey, who called his servants and entrusted his property to them. ¹⁵To one he gave five talents of money, to another two talents, and to another one talent, each according to his ability. Then he went on his journey. ¹⁶The man who had received the five talents went at once and put his money to work and gained five more. ¹⁷So also, the one with the two talents gained two more. ¹⁸But the man who had received the one talent went off, dug a hole in the ground and hid his master's money."

-Matthew 25:14-18

2. Does God have anything for me to obey?

3. Have I done anything that I need forgiveness from God for?

4. What lesson does God want me to remember this week?

Things I do not understand about this chapter...

_____

_____

_____

_____

_____

_____

Show Me the Money

Recap Your Thoughts

Just Pray

Prayer is the action of engaging your heart with the heart of God.

Talk to God

Why Not Stone Her?

weekly verse

John 8:7b

"If any one of you is without sin, let
him be the first to throw a stone at
her."

A Fully-Loaded Life

Have you ever been in an argument with another person? I'm sure you have. I have! In fact, I remember getting in this one argument with my wife over whether or not it was cool to wear sweaters. We were standing in Old Navy looking at clothes for me (since overalls were out of style for guys), and she demanded that I buy these two sweaters! Now guys, there is nothing wrong with wearing sweaters, except these particular ones were the real feminine looking ones that hugged my body tightly. They made me feel like puking. Because she claimed to be a professional "fashion consultant," she insisted I buy them. I looked at her and said, "There is no way I am spending money on these ugly sweaters I will only use as a tug-o-war rope for the dogs. I would rather wear pink underwear than these things." The truth of the matter is I was right. However, my being right did not give me the authority to slam her and her opinion. I was mean, self-centered, and rude. I was not loving, gentle, or caring. I was a punk! I did not show my wife that I loved and cared for her because I was not gentle when confronting her with my extreme dislikes!

In this lesson we are looking at gentleness and the way Jesus was gentle to a woman caught in sin. We will see that He was gentle because He sincerely loved and cared for her. Let's get on it!

***Check out Galatians 5:22 and list
"The Fruit of the Spirit" ***

_____   _____

_____   _____

_____   _____

_____   _____

_____

PREVIEW

- In your own words, define gentleness.

- Do you think gentleness has any importance in showing a person that you care for them? Why/why not?

- What do you think of when you think of a gentle person?

- Think of one way you demonstrated the character trait gentleness this past week? Explain the situation to your group. What happened? What do you think people thought of you?

First Things First

Beginning with the end in mind helps you think through the purpose of what you want to learn before you actually learn it.

FEATURE PRESENTATION

Gentleness is a character trait that is conveyed when a person truly cares, respects and loves the other person. It is not a selfish trait, and it always seeks to help or uplift the other person. If you are a person who encourages, uplifts, and praises others, then quite possibly you naturally have a gentle spirit. However, for most of us it doesn't come naturally, and we need to work on communicating our thoughts in a gentle, caring and loving way. Ask God to reveal to you what areas of your life you need help in becoming a person with a gentle and loving spirit.

A Fully-Loaded Life

Check out **John 8:1-6.**

- Why did the Jewish men bring the woman to the court?

But Jesus went to the Mount of Olives. ²At dawn he appeared again in the temple courts, where all the people gathered around him, and he sat down to teach them. ³The teachers of the law and the Pharisees brought in a woman caught in adultery. They made her stand before the group ⁴and said to Jesus, "Teacher, this woman was caught in the act of adultery. ⁵In the Law Moses commanded us to stone such women. Now what do you say?" ⁶They were using this question as a trap, in order to have a basis for accusing him.

-John 8:1-6

- Why did they only bring the woman and not the man? Who was involved in the relationship with her?

- What is the Law of Moses?

- What did these men claim it taught?

- What did they want to accuse Jesus of?

Recap Your Thoughts

_____
_____
_____
_____
_____
_____
_____
_____
_____
_____
_____
_____
_____

Prayer Model

Adore God
Confess Sins
Thank God
Supplicate
(Humbly ask
God for things)

Talk to God

_____
_____
_____
_____
_____
_____
_____
_____
_____
_____
_____
_____
_____

A Fully-Loaded Life

Read **John 8:7-8.**

- What was Jesus' reaction to the men?

> But Jesus bent down and started to write on the ground with his finger. When they kept on questioning him, he straightened up and said to them, "If any one of you is without sin, let him be the first to throw a stone at her." ⁸Again he stooped down and wrote on the ground.
>
> -John 8:7-8

- What was Jesus' response? What did Jesus tell these men?

- Why do you think Jesus was writing on the ground? What was He writing?

Recap Your Thoughts

_____
_____
_____
_____
_____
_____
_____
_____
_____
_____
_____
_____

Prayer

This is your chance to document the workings of God in your life.

Talk to God

_____
_____
_____
_____
_____
_____
_____
_____
_____
_____
_____

A Fully-Loaded Life

Check out **John 8:9-11.**

- What happened next?

> At this, those who heard began to go away one at a time, the older ones first, until only Jesus was left, with the woman still standing there. [10]Jesus straightened up and asked her, "Woman, where are they? Has no one condemned you?" [11]"No one, sir," she said. "Then neither do I condemn you," Jesus declared. "Go now and leave your life of sin."
>
> -John 8:9-11

- What is the significance of each man walking away one at a time? Why did the older ones walk away first?

- Who were the only two left?

- What question did Jesus ask the woman?

- How did Jesus demonstrate gentleness with the woman and also the men of the Law?

Recap Your Thoughts

_____
_____
_____
_____
_____
_____
_____
_____
_____
_____
_____
_____
_____
_____

Prayer

The extreme
thing about
prayer is that
God listens.

Talk to God

_____
_____
_____
_____
_____
_____
_____
_____
_____
_____
_____
_____

A Fully-Loaded Life

But Jesus went to the Mount of Olives. [2]At dawn he appeared again in the temple courts, where all the people gathered around him, and he sat down to teach them. [3]The teachers of the law and the Pharisees brought in a woman caught in adultery. They made her stand before the group [4]and said to Jesus, "Teacher, this woman was caught in the act of adultery. [5]In the Law Moses commanded us to stone such women. Now what do you say?" [6]They were using this question as a trap, in order to have a basis for accusing him. [7]But Jesus bent down and started to write on the ground with his finger. When they kept on questioning him, he straightened up and said to them, "If any one of you is without sin, let him be the first to throw a stone at her." [8]Again he stooped down and wrote on the ground. [9]At this, those who heard began to go away one at a time, the older ones first, until only Jesus was left, with the woman still standing there. [10]Jesus straightened up and asked her, "Woman, where are they? Has no one condemned you?" [11]"No one, sir," she said. "Then neither do I condemn you," Jesus declared. "Go now and leave your life of sin."

-John 8:1-11

Day Four

Reread the whole story of **John 8:1-11.**

- Why did Jesus stand up for this woman?

- Why was Jesus able to maintain His cool even when the men were attacking Him and trying to trick Him?

- What are some *key points* you can learn from Jesus' behavior and his response to both the woman and the Jewish leaders?

- When others are condemned for doing something, why is it important for us to demonstrate gentleness?

Jesus demonstrated gentleness to the woman when the Jewish leaders brought her into the temple courts by not condemning her of her sins. In His eyes all sin is equal. Furthermore, Jesus knew that every person in the temple court was a sentenced sinner, so why should they have the right to judge another? If you judge people, you cannot love them. Judging is a destructive tactic we use to build ourselves up. If you want to be a person who is gentle, caring, and loving, you must be like Jesus and not condemn others. Remember, everyone's sin is equal in God's eyes!

126

Recap Your Thoughts

_____
_____
_____
_____
_____
_____
_____
_____
_____
_____
_____
_____
_____
_____

Why Pray?

Prayer is the action of engaging your heart with the heart of God.

Talk to God

_____
_____
_____
_____
_____
_____
_____
_____
_____
_____
_____

Day Five

CREDITS

1. How can you be more like Jesus this week?

2. How can you begin to develop a gentle heart?

3. List some ways you judge people.
   a)
   b)
   c)
   d)

The credits section is designed to help you apply this week's chapter to your life. It can also be used for further discussion in a small group setting.

4. Now list some ways you can stop judging people.
   a)
   b)
   c)
   d)

5. What happens when we judge others?

6. After this lesson, how would you define gentleness to someone?

7. Are you capable of being a gentle person if you are negative, judgmental, and destructive consistantly? Why/why not?

Recap Your Thoughts

_____
_____
_____
_____
_____
_____
_____
_____
_____
_____
_____
_____
_____
_____

Why Pray?

A fully-loaded life centers on the reality that prayer works.

Talk to God

_____
_____
_____
_____
_____
_____
_____
_____
_____
_____
_____
_____
_____

A Fully-Loaded Life

MEMORY VERSE

"If any one of you is without sin, let him be the first to throw a stone at her."

- John 8:7b

Living It Out

As a Junior High student, it is time to begin to live your faith out rather than strictly filling yourself up with knowledge. By focusing on one verse weekly, you're given the chance to put into practice what you have been studying. It's up to you to live it out!

How can I apply this lesson to my life?

How can I apply this lesson at school?

Recap Your Thoughts

_____
_____
_____
_____
_____
_____
_____
_____
_____
_____
_____
_____
_____
_____
_____
_____

Why Pray?

God moves in big ways when students are led to pray.

Talk to God

_____
_____
_____
_____
_____
_____
_____
_____
_____
_____
_____
_____
_____
_____

A Fully-Loaded Life

REWIND

1. What has God promised me this week?

2. Does God have anything for me to obey?

Keeping It Real

But Jesus bent down and started to write on the ground with his finger. When they kept on questioning him, he straightened up and said to them, "If any one of you is without sin, let him be the first to throw a stone at her." ⁸Again he stooped down and wrote on the ground.

-John 8:7-8

3. Have I done anything that I need forgiveness from God for?

4. What lesson does God want me to remember this week?

Things I do not understand about this chapter...

_____

_____

_____

_____

_____

_____

Recap Your Thoughts

_____
_____
_____
_____
_____
_____
_____
_____
_____
_____
_____
_____
_____
_____

Just Pray

Prayer is our channel to dialogue with God whenever and wherever we'd like.

Talk to God

_____
_____
_____
_____
_____
_____
_____
_____
_____
_____
_____
_____

Self What?

A Fully-Loaded Life

TRAILER

I remember when I was in the eleventh grade I had a friend who wanted to skip out of school. He wanted to take a trip up to the mountains and hangout. He asked me if I'd go with him. This proposal sounded very appealing. I had never ditched school before, and I always liked a little danger in my life (it helped me to know I was alive). He begged and pleaded with me telling me that no one would find out and everything would be alright. I gave in! I ditched school and drove up to the mountains with him. We hung out all day doing absolutely nothing. It was great! Thinking back on that onetime experience, though, I recognize that what I did was wrong. I lied to my parents, teachers, and friends about where I was all day. My friend was right, no one found out what I did (until now), but I felt horrible! If only I had the self-control to say no to my buddy, I would not have had to live all these years with this lie.

In this lesson we are talking about self-control. We will look at a story where Jesus was tempted three times by Satan, but had enough self-control not to give in. As you read this account from the Bible, think to yourself whether or not you could have the same amount of self-control Jesus did. Then ask yourself why/why not?

***Check out Galatians 5:22 and list
"The Fruit of the Spirit" ***

_____   _____
_____   _____
_____   _____
_____   _____
_____

Self What?

PREVIEW

- Did you show self-control at all this last week? How?

First Things First

Beginning with the end in mind helps you think through the purpose of what you want to learn before you actually learn it.

- What is the one area of your life you lack self-control in? How do you deal with it? How will you change?

- Would your friends say that you are a person who has self-control? Why/why not?

FEATURE PRESENTATION

As a Christian, your friends watch the way you act. They know, or at least expect, a Christian should act a certain way. The Bible calls you to be a good witness to everyone you are around. This means controlling your actions and attitudes. You can either lead a person to Christ with your actions and attitudes, or turn them away from Christ. The choice is yours; however, God wants you to lead them to Him, and if you are going to do so, you must practice self-control! Ask God to reveal to you any area of your life you need self-control in.

A Fully-Loaded Life

Check out **Luke 4:1-2.**

- Where was Jesus?

Jesus, full of the Holy Spirit, returned from the Jordan and was led by the Spirit in the desert, ²where for forty days he was tempted by the devil. He ate nothing during those days, and at the end of them he was hungry.

-Luke 4:1-2

- How long did Jesus go without food?

- In your own words describe what you think being "led by the Holy Spirit" means.

- What was the very first thing Jesus had to have self-control not to do? Do you think it would be hard? Could you do it?

Recap Your Thoughts

_____
_____
_____
_____
_____
_____
_____
_____
_____
_____
_____
_____
_____
_____

Fully Loaded

Acquiring God's presence in our lives daily is the first step towards achieving a fully loaded life.

Talk to God

_____
_____
_____
_____
_____
_____
_____
_____
_____
_____
_____
_____

A Fully-Loaded Life

Check out **Luke 4:3-4.**

- How did the devil tempt Jesus?

The devil said to him, "If you are the Son of God, tell this stone to become bread." ⁴Jesus answered, "It is written: 'Man does not live on bread alone.'"

-Luke 4:3-4

- How did Jesus respond?

- How did Jesus demonstrate self-control?

- Why do you think Satan was tempting Jesus? What did he want to see happen/accomplished?

Recap Your Thoughts

_____

_____

_____

_____

_____

_____

_____

_____

_____

_____

_____

_____

_____

Extreme Joy

God wants each of us to do everything joyfully, without complaining, as if we were doing it for Him directly.

Talk to God

_____

_____

_____

_____

_____

_____

_____

_____

_____

_____

_____

A Fully-Loaded Life

Read **Luke 4:5-8.**

- What happened in these verses?

The devil led him up to a high place and showed him in an instant all the kingdoms of the world. ⁶And he said to him, "I will give you all their authority and splendor, for it has been given to me, and I can give it to anyone I want to. ⁷So if you worship me, it will all be yours." ⁸Jesus answered, "It is written: 'Worship the Lord your God and serve him only.'"

-Luke 4:5-8

- Do you think Jesus was tempted at all with this? Why/why not?

- Do you think Satan was scared to even try to tempt Jesus? Do you think that before he tempted Jesus he had second thoughts? Why/why not?

- How did Jesus respond?

Self What?

_____
_____
_____
_____
_____
_____
_____
_____
_____
_____
_____
_____
_____
_____

Prayer

We all should pray in such a way that we demonstrate an authentic humility before God.

Talk to God

_____
_____
_____
_____
_____
_____
_____
_____
_____
_____
_____
_____
_____

A Fully-Loaded Life

Jesus, full of the Holy Spirit, returned from the Jordan and was led by the Spirit in the desert, ²where for forty days he was tempted by the devil. He ate nothing during those days, and at the end of them he was hungry. ³The devil said to him, "If you are the Son of God, tell this stone to become bread." ⁴Jesus answered, "It is written: 'Man does not live on bread alone.'" ⁵The devil led him up to a high place and showed him in an instant all the kingdoms of the world. ⁶And he said to him, "I will give you all their authority and splendor, for it has been given to me, and I can give it to anyone I want to. ⁷So if you worship me, it will all be yours." ⁸Jesus answered, "It is written: 'Worship the Lord your God and serve him only.'" ⁹The devil led him to Jerusalem and had him stand on the highest point of the temple. "If you are the Son of God," he said, "throw yourself down from here. ¹⁰For it is written: 'He will command his angels concerning you to guard you carefully; ¹¹they will lift you up in their hands, so that you will not strike your foot against a stone.'"¹²Jesus answered, "It says: 'Do not put the Lord your God to the test.'" ¹³When the devil had finished all this tempting, he left him until an opportune time.

-Luke 4:1-13

Read the whole story from **Luke 4:1-13**.

• How did Satan tempt Jesus a third time?

• What was Jesus' response?

• Do you think Jesus demonstrated self-control during all three temptations? Why/why not?

• How did Jesus counter Satan's temptations?

• Do you think you can have as much self-control over your daily temptations as Jesus did in this story?

Recap Your Thoughts

_____
_____
_____
_____
_____
_____
_____
_____
_____
_____
_____
_____

Prayer Model

Adoration,
Confession,
Thanksgiving
and
Supplication
are four aspects
of prayer that
each of us must
have in order to
live a fully-
loaded life for
Christ.

Talk to God

_____
_____
_____
_____
_____
_____
_____
_____
_____
_____
_____

A Fully-Loaded Life

CREDITS

1. What do you think would have happened to Jesus if He gave in to Satan and his temptations?

2. List three ways you will begin to have self-control over the next week.
   a)
   b)
   c)

The credits section is designed to help you apply this week's chapter to your life. It can also be used for further discussion in a small group setting.

3. Write out and memorize **1 Corinthians 10:13.**

4. How does memorizing this verse make you feel?

5. How does memorizing this verse allow you to maintain better self-control when you're tempted?

Remember: God wants you to be a witness to everyone. Satan will try and screw that witness up by tempting you to do things you normally wouldn't do! If you can maintain self-control like Jesus did in the desert, your witness will rock your school, friends, sport teams, etc. Just keep in mind 1 Corinthians 10:13.

Self What?

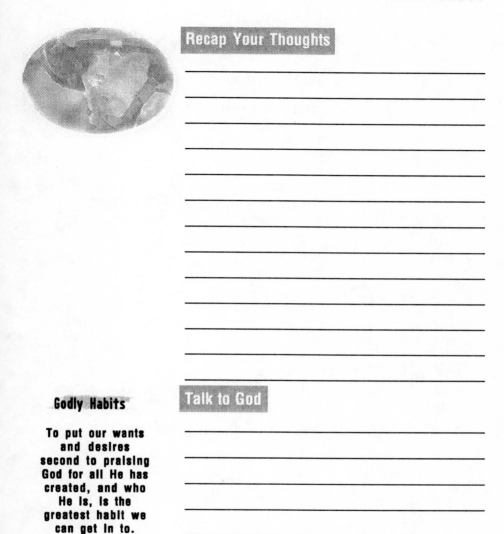

Recap Your Thoughts

Godly Habits

To put our wants and desires second to praising God for all He has created, and who He is, is the greatest habit we can get in to.

Talk to God

A Fully-Loaded Life

MEMORY VERSE

Jesus answered, "It is written: 'Worship the Lord your God and serve him only.'"

-Luke 4:8

Living It Out

As a Junior High student, It Is time to begin to live your faith out rather than strictly filling yourself up with knowledge. By focusing on one verse weekly, you're given the chance to put Into practice what you have been studying. It's up to you to live It out!

How can I apply this lesson to my life?

How can I apply this lesson at school?

Recap Your Thoughts

_____
_____
_____
_____
_____
_____
_____
_____
_____
_____
_____
_____
_____
_____

Attitude Check

Our attitudes, however, are the one thing we always have the ability to control.

Talk to God

_____
_____
_____
_____
_____
_____
_____
_____
_____
_____
_____

A Fully-Loaded Life

REWIND

1. What has God promised me this week?

Keeping It Real

2. Does God have anything for me to obey?

The devil led him up to a high place and showed him in an instant all the kingdoms of the world. ⁶And he said to him, "I will give you all their authority and splendor, for it has been given to me, and I can give it to anyone I want to. ⁷So if you worship me, it will all be yours." ⁸Jesus answered, "It is written: 'Worship the Lord your God and serve him only.'"

-Luke 4:5-8

3. Have I done anything that I need forgiveness from God for?

4. What lesson does God want me to remember this week?

Things I do not understand about this chapter...

_____

_____

_____

_____

_____

_____

Self What?

Recap Your Thoughts

_____
_____
_____
_____
_____
_____
_____
_____
_____
_____
_____
_____
_____
_____

Adore God

To adore God means to give God authentic praise for His creativity and power over all creation.

Talk to God

_____
_____
_____
_____
_____
_____
_____
_____
_____
_____
_____

chapter nine

Drowning in Fear

weekly verse

Matthew 14:31
Immediately Jesus reached out his hand and caught him. "You of little faith," he said, "why did you doubt?"

TRAILER

Think of your worst fear. Tell your group what it is and why you are so scared of it. When I think of my worst fear I would have to say it would be the fear of drowning. I have a huge fear of water. I think it all started when I was a Junior in High School. I was going "spelunking" (caving for the lay person). The cave I was going to was over a two mile hike through tall brush and jagged rocks. I got this brilliant idea of jumping into the river that ran parallel to the hiking path and taking a leisurely float right down to the cave spot. So I jumped, fully-clothed, right into the water that looked so calm, shoes and everything. I was having a blast for about the first twenty feet. After that, I found out the water wasn't calm at all. In fact, there were rapids like I've never seen before hiding right behind a bend in the riverbank. Fear welled up inside me, and I felt like I was going to drown. I was being pulled under and over rocks. I was in a major jam. I began to swim as hard as I could to the side of the river. After around thirty minutes of fighting the twenty-knot current, I surfaced on a sandy beach breathing with relief that I was safe. That was one day I will never forget!

That day scarred me for life and eternally gave me a fear of water. Thinking about my foolish decision to jump into the freezing cold river gave me a new perspective on what it must have been like for Peter when he began to drown after walking towards Jesus on the water. For the first time, that story had a new meaning for me. For the first time in my life I experienced, much like Peter, total fear.

In this chapter we are talking about fear. We will look at a story where Jesus walked on water. We will see that His disciples became fearful. We want to see how Jesus tells us to deal with our fear! What should we do when we get scared?

PREVIEW

- What are you most scared of? Why does this scare you?

First Things First

Beginning with the end in mind helps you think through the purpose of what you want to learn before you actually learn it.

- Do you think Jesus wants you to be scared? Why/ why not?

- As a Christian, shouldn't you be fearless? Why/ why not?

- Tell your group one thing you are most scared of that is going to happen to you this next week or month.

FEATURE PRESENTATION

I Peter 5:7

As a Christian, God does not want you to live in fear. God designed you to praise and worship Him. Satan knows this. He also knows that if he can bog you down with fear, then you will be useless to furthering God's kingdom. You must understand that God controls those things we are most scared of. In fact, God wants you to "cast all your fears on Him because He cares for you!" Isn't that cool? God wants to take your fear from you. Jesus has called you to put your total faith in Him, trusting that He will protect you and care for you. Before you begin this week's study ask God to release you from any fear you may be dealing with. Ask God to confirm in your heart that He is in control and is watching out for your best interests!

A Fully-Loaded Life

Check out **Matthew 14:22-24.**

- Where did Jesus go after He dismissed the crowd?

Immediately Jesus made the disciples get into the boat and go on ahead of him to the other side, while he dismissed the crowd. 23After he had dismissed them, he went up on a mountainside by himself to pray. When evening came, he was there alone, 24but the boat was already a considerable distance from land, buffeted by the waves because the wind was against it.

-Matthew 14:22-24

- Why was Jesus alone? What is the importance of us spending time alone with God?

- Is prayer one way you can praise and worship God? Why/why not?

Recap Your Thoughts

_____
_____
_____
_____
_____
_____
_____
_____
_____
_____
_____
_____
_____

Why Pray?

When we pray to God, we are communicating with the most powerful being ever.

- Dustin Heiner

Talk to God

_____
_____
_____
_____
_____
_____
_____
_____
_____
_____
_____
_____

A Fully-Loaded Life

Check out **Matthew 14:25-26.**

- **What did Jesus do next?**

During the fourth watch of the night Jesus went out to them, walking on the lake. ²⁶When the disciples saw him walking on the lake, they were terrified. "It's a ghost," they said, and cried out in fear.

-Matthew   14:25-26

- **Why did His disciples get so scared?**

- **What would you have done if you were on that boat with the disciples?**

Recap Your Thoughts

_____
_____
_____
_____
_____
_____
_____
_____
_____
_____
_____
_____
_____
_____

Prayer

This is your chance to document the workings of God in your life.

Talk to God

_____
_____
_____
_____
_____
_____
_____
_____
_____
_____
_____
_____

A Fully-Loaded Life

Read **Matthew 14:27-29.**

- What happened in these verses?

But Jesus immediately said to them: "Take courage! It is I. Don't be afraid." 28"Lord, if it's you," Peter replied, "tell me to come to you on the water." 29"Come," he said.

-Matthew 14:27-29

- Why did Jesus tell His disciples not to be afraid? Do think they listened or questioned?

- What happened with Peter?

- What is so significant about Peter walking on water?

- Was Peter reacting to Jesus in faith? Why/why not?

Recap Your Thoughts

_____
_____
_____
_____
_____
_____
_____
_____
_____
_____
_____
_____
_____
_____

Prayer Warrior

It takes a person with an extremely Godly character to live a life of authentic prayer.

Talk to God

_____
_____
_____
_____
_____
_____
_____
_____
_____
_____
_____

A Fully-Loaded Life

Immediately Jesus made the disciples get into the boat and go on ahead of him to the other side, while he dismissed the crowd. ²³After he had dismissed them, he went up on a mountainside by himself to pray. When evening came, he was there alone, ²⁴but the boat was already a considerable distance from land, buffeted by the waves because the wind was against it. ²⁵During the fourth watch of the night Jesus went out to them, walking on the lake. ²⁶When the disciples saw him walking on the lake, they were terrified. "It's a ghost," they said, and cried out in fear. ²⁷But Jesus immediately said to them: "Take courage! It is I. Don't be afraid." ²⁸"Lord, if it's you," Peter replied, "tell me to come to you on the water." ²⁹"Come," he said. ³⁰Then Peter got down out of the boat, walked on the water and came toward Jesus. But when he saw the wind, he was afraid and, beginning to sink, cried out, "Lord, save me!" ³¹Immediately Jesus reached out his hand and caught him. "You of little faith," he said, "why did you doubt?" ³²And when they climbed into the boat, the wind died down. ³³Then those who were in the boat worshiped him, saying, "Truly you are the Son of God."

-Matthew 14:22-32

Read the whole story from **Matthew 14:22-32.**

• What happened when Peter saw the wind?

• What did Jesus say to Peter?

• How does this story of Jesus calming the storm and walking on water teach you not to be fearful?

• Are you kind of like Peter? Are you sort of putting your trust in Jesus with your minor situations, but when the major storms start up you don't trust Him?

Recap Your Thoughts

_____
_____
_____
_____
_____
_____
_____
_____
_____
_____
_____
_____

My Direct Line

Prayer is the line we connect to in order for God to give us that extra touch of love.

Talk to God

_____
_____
_____
_____
_____
_____
_____
_____
_____
_____
_____

A Fully-Loaded Life

CREDITS

1. What must you do to develop trust in Jesus and have faith that He will watch over you and cause you to stop fearing all the scary things in life?

2. List three ways you will begin to build your faith in Jesus over the next week:
   a)
   b)
   c)

The credits section is designed to help you apply this week's chapter to your life. It can also be used for further discussion in a small group setting.

3. Write out and memorize **1 Peter 5:7.**

4. How does this verse make you feel?

5. What does this verse tell you that Jesus wants you to do when you are scared or have many burdens?

Remember: God loves you! I know sometimes He puts trials in your life, which cause you to wonder if He really does, but you must not ever forget that He will never leave you nor abandon you. This is His promise to you! So, no matter how scared you get, you can always fall back on this awesome promise. When fear comes, pray hard for faith! Don't be like Peter who doubted God. Instead, know and willingly rely on Him to bring you through. In prayer, praise God for all the ways He has watched over you already and will continue to do so in the future.

Recap Your Thoughts

_____
_____
_____
_____
_____
_____
_____
_____
_____
_____
_____
_____
_____
_____
_____

Got Jesus?

God wants one thing from you... Your life.

Talk to God

_____
_____
_____
_____
_____
_____
_____
_____
_____
_____
_____
_____

Day Six

MEMORY VERSE

Immediately Jesus reached out his hand and caught him. "You of little faith," he said, "why did you doubt?"

- Matthew 14:31

Living It Out

As a Junior High student, it is time to begin to live your faith out rather than strictly filling yourself up with knowledge. By focusing on one verse weekly, you're given the chance to put into practice what you have been studying. It's up to you to live it out!

How can I apply this lesson to my life?

How can I apply this lesson at school?

Recap Your Thoughts

_____
_____
_____
_____
_____
_____
_____
_____
_____
_____
_____
_____
_____
_____
_____
_____

God Listens

God is willing to listen to us; however, we must understand and believe that God's will may be different from our own.

Talk to God

_____
_____
_____
_____
_____
_____
_____
_____
_____
_____
_____
_____

A Fully-Loaded Life

REWIND

1. What has God promised me this week?

Keeping It Real

But Jesus immediately said to them: "Take courage! It is I. Don't be afraid." 28"Lord, if it's you," Peter replied, "tell me to come to you on the water." 29"Come," he said.

-Matthew 14:27-29

2. Does God have anything for me to obey?

3. Have I done anything that I need forgiveness from God for?

4. What lesson does God want me to remember this week?

Things I do not understand about this chapter...

_____

_____

_____

_____

_____

_____

Recap Your Thoughts

Adore God

To adore God means to give God authentic praise for His creativity and power over all creation.

Talk to God

chapter ten

The Miraculous Catch

weekly verse

Luke 5:11
Then Jesus said to Simon, "Don't be afraid; from now on you will catch men."

A Fully-Loaded Life

TRAILER

Have you ever been fishing? I love to fish. In fact, I remember when I was in eigth grade my parents let me go with three of my friends up to the mountains for a weekend fishing trip—alone! It was awesome. We packed up the suburban with every kind of tackle and bait imaginable. We loaded our camping stove, sleeping bags, inflatable raft, food, wood, and many extras. We were totally stoked to be going fishing alone. When we arrived at our camp spot two hours later, my friend's dad dropped us off and then went back down the mountain. We were totally alone. I mean we had to cook our own food, rig our own showers, tie our own hooks onto our fishing line: we were living it up as men! Like I said, this was not just a camping trip, but a fishing trip. We all woke up early every morning and fished from 4:00 am to 6:00 PM. Unfortunately, despite the fact we had spent a ton of money on bait, it was not enough. At the end of a very long fishing weekend, we had only the holes in our sleeping bags from the ashes of the fire to show for our efforts: we had been skunked! That means we went home with zero fish. We spent hours fishing and caught nothing. We were totally bummed!

Well, my friend's dad came back up on Sunday to pick us up. We were all so embarrassed to tell him we caught nothing. But, like men, we sucked up our pride and bit the bullet. We told him, and he laughed hysterically. That weekend taught me a lot. First, it taught me that I was not cut out to be a fisherman. Second, I learned that fishing was way harder than it looked. Third, now when I read a fishing story from the Bible I can empathize with the characters who fished for a living but went days without food because they had caught nothing. In fact, through this whole experience, I began to think about Simon from the Bible and the story where he and his boys were fishing all night and caught nothing. In the morning, Jesus told him to throw his net in the water. When Simon did this his net tore because of all the fish, and he fell at Jesus' feet asking forgiveness for questioning Him and not believing.

In this lesson, we are talking about fishing. We are not referring to fish fishing, but people fishing. We are going to look at the Biblical account of Simon throwing his net in the water, and Jesus giving him the best fishing experience of his life. We will also discuss how to apply this story to our everyday junior high lives. Let's get into it!

PREVIEW

- Do you ever question God? Have you ever known the right thing to do, or something that you should do, but you questioned or just didn't do it? If so, what was it and why did you question?

- Do you believe that God cares for you? How about others? Why/why not?

- What is the first thing you must do if you are going to fish for Jesus?

- What kind of fishing do you think you're called to do as a Christian? Do you do it? Why/why not?

- Do you find it hard to fish the way Jesus wants you to? What is the hardest thing about it?

First Things First

Beginning with the end in mind helps you think through the purpose of what you want to learn before you actually learn it.

FEATURE PRESENTATION

As a Christian, you are called to be a fisher of men. I know this is a very difficult thing to do. Exactly what does "fisher of men" mean? It means that as a Christian you are telling your friends about Jesus and giving them a chance to respond. It is very much like fishing in that you must put bait out for your friends, such as questions and prayer, and wait for them to take hold. God wants you on His boat. Just like He called Simon as you will see shortly, so He has also called you! However, just like Simon, you must be willing to give up everything and follow Him. Before you begin this lesson, ask God to reveal to you anything that blocks you from fully following Him. Ask Him to touch your heart for your friends. Ask Him to make you a fisherman like Simon.

173

A Fully-Loaded Life

Check out **Luke 5:1-4.**

- What does the passage say Jesus was doing?

One day as Jesus was standing by the Lake of Gennesaret, with the people crowding around him and listening to the word of God, ²he saw at the water's edge two boats, left there by the fishermen, who were washing their nets. ³He got into one of the boats, the one belonging to Simon, and asked him to put out a little from shore. Then he sat down and taught the people from the boat. ⁴When he had finished speaking, he said to Simon, "Put out into deep water, and let down the nets for a catch."

-Luke 5:1-4

- Did you know that the Sea of Galilee is also know as the Lake of Gennesaret?

- Why do you think the fishermen were washing their nets? Would it be important for their nets to stay clean?

- When Jesus was done speaking, what did He tell Simon to do?

- In your opinion, **without reading ahead**, what is the significance of this demand?

The Miraculous Catch

_____
_____
_____
_____
_____
_____
_____
_____
_____
_____
_____
_____
_____

Prayer Model

Adore God
Confess Sins
Thank God
Supplicate
(Humbly ask
God for things)

Talk to God

_____
_____
_____
_____
_____
_____
_____
_____
_____
_____
_____

A Fully-Loaded Life

Check out **Luke 5:5-7.**

- How did Simon respond to Jesus' demand?

⁵Simon answered, "Master, we've worked hard all night and haven't caught anything. But because you say so, I will let down the nets." ⁶When they had done so, they caught such a large number of fish that their nets began to break. ⁷So they signaled their partners in the other boat to come and help them, and they came and filled both boats so full that they began to sink.

-Luke 5:5-7

- Write out what your "honest" response would have been if you were in Simon's shoes.

- What was the significance of Jesus' demand? In your opinion, what was Jesus' main reason for performing this miracle?

Recap Your Thoughts

_____
_____
_____
_____
_____
_____
_____
_____
_____
_____
_____
_____
_____
_____

Prayer

This is your chance to document the workings of God in your life.

Talk to God

_____
_____
_____
_____
_____
_____
_____
_____
_____
_____
_____
_____

A Fully-Loaded Life

Read **Luke 5:8-10.**

- What happened in these verses?

When Simon Peter saw this, he fell at Jesus' knees and said, "Go away from me, Lord; I am a sinful man!" ⁹For he and all his companions were astonished at the catch of fish they had taken, ¹⁰and so were James and John, the sons of Zebedee, Simon's partners.

-Luke 5:8-10

- Why did Simon fall on his knees?

- What is the significance of Simon falling to his knees?

- What must you do when you disobey God? Was Simon asking for forgiveness?

- Has God ever blessed you when you thought there was no hope? If so, what happened? How did you feel? How big did God seem at that point?

Recap Your Thoughts

_____
_____
_____
_____
_____
_____
_____
_____
_____
_____
_____
_____
_____
_____
_____

Prayer

The extreme
thing about
prayer is that
God listens.

Talk to God

_____
_____
_____
_____
_____
_____
_____
_____
_____
_____
_____
_____
_____

A Fully-Loaded Life

One day as Jesus was standing by the Lake of Gennesaret, with the people crowding around him and listening to the word of God, ²he saw at the water's edge two boats, left there by the fishermen, who were washing their nets. ³He got into one of the boats, the one belonging to Simon, and asked him to put out a little from shore. Then he sat down and taught the people from the boat. ⁴When he had finished speaking, he said to Simon, "Put out into deep water, and let down the nets for a catch." ⁵Simon answered, "Master, we've worked hard all night and haven't caught anything. But because you say so, I will let down the nets." ⁶When they had done so, they caught such a large number of fish that their nets began to break. ⁷So they signaled their partners in the other boat to come and help them, and they came and filled both boats so full that they began to sink. ⁸When Simon Peter saw this, he fell at Jesus' knees and said, "Go away from me, Lord; I am a sinful man!" ⁹For he and all his companions were astonished at the catch of fish they had taken, ¹⁰and so were James and John, the sons of Zebedee, Simon's partners. ¹¹Then Jesus said to Simon, "Don't be afraid; from now on you will catch men." So they pulled their boats up on shore, left everything and followed him.

-Luke 5:1-11

Read the whole story from **Luke 5:1-11.**

- What did Jesus say to Simon at the end of the day?

- What did Jesus mean when He said, "...from now on you will catch men+?"

- Did Simon go with Jesus? What did he do with all his fishing gear and boats?

- Are you like Simon? Is God calling you to fish for your friends? How are you responding?

Recap Your Thoughts

_____
_____
_____
_____
_____
_____
_____
_____
_____
_____
_____
_____
_____
_____
_____

Why Pray?

Prayer is the action of engaging your heart with the heart of God.

Talk to God

_____
_____
_____
_____
_____
_____
_____
_____
_____
_____
_____
_____

A Fully-Loaded Life

CREDITS

1. How are you going to be like Simon this week?

2. List some ways you think God can speak to you.
   a)
   b)
   c)

The credits section is designed to help you apply this week's chapter to your life. It can also be used for further discussion in a small group setting.

3. How are you going to respond when God calls on you to trust Him?

4. List some areas in your life where you need to put your trust in Jesus.
   a)
   b)
   c)
   d)
   e)

5. List some things God is asking you to give up to catch your friends.
   a)
   b)
   c)
   d)

Recap Your Thoughts

_____
_____
_____
_____
_____
_____
_____
_____
_____
_____
_____
_____
_____

Why Pray?

A fully-loaded life centers on the reality that prayer works.

Talk to God

_____
_____
_____
_____
_____
_____
_____
_____
_____
_____

A Fully-Loaded Life

MEMORY VERSE

Then Jesus said to Simon, "Don't be afraid; from now on you will catch men."

- Luke 5:10

How can I apply this lesson to my life?

Living It Out

As a Junior High student, it is time to begin to live your faith out rather than strictly filling yourself up with knowledge. By focusing on one verse weekly, you're given the chance to put into practice what you have been studying. It's up to you to live it out!

.

How can I apply this lesson at school?

Recap Your Thoughts

_____
_____
_____
_____
_____
_____
_____
_____
_____
_____
_____
_____
_____

Why Pray?

God moves in
big ways when
students
pray.

Talk to God

_____
_____
_____
_____
_____
_____
_____
_____
_____
_____
_____
_____

A Fully-Loaded Life

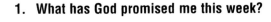
REWIND

1. What has God promised me this week?

Keeping It Real

One day as Jesus was standing by the Lake of Gennesaret, with the people crowding around him and listening to the word of God, ²he saw at the water's edge two boats, left there by the fishermen, who were washing their nets. ³He got into one of the boats, the one belonging to Simon, and asked him to put out a little from shore. Then he sat down and taught the people from the boat. ⁴When he had finished speaking, he said to Simon, "Put out into deep water, and let down the nets for a catch."

-Luke 5:1-4

2. Does God have anything for me to obey?

3. Have I done anything that I need forgiveness from God for?

4. What lesson does God want me to remember this week?

Things I do not understand about this chapter...

_____

_____

_____

_____

_____

_____

Recap Your Thoughts

_____
_____
_____
_____
_____
_____
_____
_____
_____
_____
_____
_____
_____

Just Pray

Prayer is our channel to dialogue with God whenever and wherever we'd like.

Talk to God

_____
_____
_____
_____
_____
_____
_____
_____
_____
_____
_____

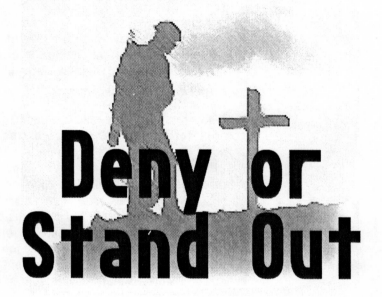

chapter eleven

Deny or Stand Out

weekly verse

Mark 14:72

Immediately the rooster crowed the second time. Then Peter remembered the word Jesus had spoken to him: "Before the rooster crows twice you will disown me three times." And he broke down and wept.

A Fully-Loaded Life

TRAILER

Have you ever been at school and had one of your friends or a person who is really popular come up to you and say, "Dude, you're one of those Jesus lovers, aren't you?" If you haven't, I can assure you that if you are living like we talked about in our last chapter, as a person who wants to reel people in and show them the love of Jesus, you will! There is definitely going to be a "defining moment" in your life where you are going to either deny Christ or stand out for Christ!

In this lesson, we are talking about being a "stand out" for Christ, regardless of the pressure surrounding you. We are going to look at the Biblical account where Peter, one of Jesus' disciples, is hanging out in a courtyard where the soldiers took Jesus after He was arrested. You will see how Peter did not have the courage to stand up for his Lord Jesus. He folded under pressure for fear of what might happen to his own life. This week is a defining moment for you to either decide to stand out for Christ or be like Peter and deny Him! Let's go after it!

***Check out Galatians 5:22 and list "The Fruit of the Spirit" ***

_____   _____
_____   _____
_____   _____
_____   _____
_____

PREVIEW

- Define the word "deny."

First Things First

Beginning with the end in mind helps you think through the purpose of what you want to learn before you actually learn it.

- Have you ever told another person at your school or anywhere else that you do not know Jesus?

- Have you ever found yourself caught in a lie where you deny your involvement with Jesus and Church? If so, explain what happened.

- How did you feel after telling your friends, family members, teachers, etc. that you did not know Jesus?

FEATURE PRESENTATION

As a Christian, Christ calls you to stand out for Him. He doesn't want babies on His sidelines, He wants warriors. Jesus wants you to learn from Peter and his weakness. He does not want you to experience the same level of pain that Peter felt after denying His involvement with and knowledge of His Lord. Jesus has not made you a wimp! Did you know that Jesus has made you strong, smart, good looking, and cute so you can stand out for Him? Ask God right now to show you times in your own life where you have denied Him. Ask for His forgiveness, and then ask Him to make you strong so that you stand out for Him on your campus.

A Fully-Loaded Life

Check out **Mark 14:66-68.**

- What happens in these verses?

While Peter was below in the courtyard, one of the servant girls of the high priest came by. 67When she saw Peter warming himself, she looked closely at him. "You also were with that Nazarene, Jesus," she said. 68But he denied it. "I don't know or understand what you're talking about," he said, and went out into the entryway.

-Mark 14:66-68

- Who was Peter talking to?

- Why do you think Peter would care about what a servant girl thought?

- Write out the words Peter used in his first denial.

- What is the significance of Peter telling the woman he didn't know Jesus?

Deny or Stand Out

Recap Your Thoughts

_____
_____
_____
_____
_____
_____
_____
_____
_____
_____
_____
_____
_____
_____

Fully Loaded

Acquiring God's presence in our lives daily is the first step towards achieving a fully loaded life.

Talk to God

_____
_____
_____
_____
_____
_____
_____
_____
_____
_____
_____
_____

A Fully-Loaded Life

Read **Mark 14:69-70.**

- Where did Peter go after the girl made her first accusation?

When the servant girl saw him there, she said again to those standing around, "This fellow is one of them." [70]Again he denied It. After a little while, those standing near said to Peter, "Surely you are one of them, for you are a Galilean."

-Mark 14:69-70

- Who made the second accusation? Do you think she was following him?

- Why do you think she talked to the crowd around Peter the second time instead of directly to him?

- What happened when she made the crowd aware of who Peter was?

- Do you think Peter was getting scared? Why/why not? Why might Peter have been afraid?

Recap Your Thoughts

_____
_____
_____
_____
_____
_____
_____
_____
_____
_____
_____
_____

Extreme Joy

God wants each of us to do everything joyfully, without complaining, as if we were doing it for Him directly.

Talk to God

_____
_____
_____
_____
_____
_____
_____
_____
_____
_____
_____

A Fully-Loaded Life

Check out Peter's reaction in **Mark 14:71.**

- What did Peter do when the crowd shouted at him?

He began to call down curses on himself, and he swore to them, "I don't know this man you're talking about."

-Mark 14:71

- Write out Peter's third denial.

*Did you know: Peter's cursing was more than just cussing? Peter was actually denying with an oath that he knew Jesus. This means he was actually saying, "May God strike me dead if I'm lying" (NIV, Life Application Study Bible, 1173)."

- Have you ever done something like this? Have you ever wanted to be accepted by the popular crowd or sport "jocks" so much that you denied your faith and left Jesus hangin'? How did it make you feel? What kind of witness were you?

Recap Your Thoughts

_____
_____
_____
_____
_____
_____
_____
_____
_____
_____
_____
_____
_____

Prayer

We all should pray In such a way that we demonstrate an authentic humility before God.

Talk to God

_____
_____
_____
_____
_____
_____
_____
_____
_____
_____
_____

A Fully-Loaded Life

Read the whole story from **Mark 14:66-72.**

While Peter was below in the courtyard, one of the servant girls of the high priest came by. ⁶⁷When she saw Peter warming himself, she looked closely at him. "You also were with that Nazarene, Jesus," she said. ⁶⁸But he denied it. "I don't know or understand what you're talking about," he said, and went out into the entryway. ⁶⁹When the servant girl saw him there, she said again to those standing around, "This fellow is one of them." ⁷⁰Again he denied it. After a little while, those standing near said to Peter, "Surely you are one of them, for you are a Galilean." ⁷¹He began to call down curses on himself, and he swore to them, "I don't know this man you're talking about." ⁷²Immediately the rooster crowed the second time. Then Peter remembered the word Jesus had spoken to him: "Before the rooster crows twice you will disown me three times." And he broke down and wept.

-Mark 14:66-72

- What happened after the third denial?

- What was Peter's decision, did he deny or stand out for Christ?

- How could he have stood out? List some of your own ideas.

- How do you think Peter's denial made Jesus feel?

Recap Your Thoughts

_____

_____

_____

_____

_____

_____

_____

_____

_____

_____

_____

_____

Prayer Model

Adoration,
Confession,
Thanksgiving
and
Supplication
are four aspects
of prayer that
each of us must
practice in
order to live a
fully-loaded life
for Christ.

Talk to God

_____

_____

_____

_____

_____

_____

_____

_____

_____

_____

_____

A Fully-Loaded Life

CREDITS

1. What do you plan to do when confronted with a hard decision to stand up for Jesus?

The credits section is designed to help you apply this week's chapter to your life. It can also be used for further discussion in a small group setting.

2. List some ways you can stand up for Jesus.
   a)
   b)
   c)
   d)

3. Make a covenant between you and God. Write out in your own words your promise to not leave Him hanging when your friends think He's uncool. Tell God what you are going to do, then sign and date it.

X_____ Date

Recap Your Thoughts

_____
_____
_____
_____
_____
_____
_____
_____
_____
_____
_____
_____
_____

Godly Habits

To put our wants and desires second to praising God for all He has created, and who He is, is the greatest habit we can get in to.

Talk to God

_____
_____
_____
_____
_____
_____
_____
_____
_____
_____
_____
_____
_____

A Fully-Loaded Life

MEMORY VERSE

Immediately the rooster crowed the second time. Then Peter remembered the word Jesus had spoken to him: "Before the rooster crows twice you will disown me three times." And he broke down and wept.

- Mark 14:72

Living It Out

As a Junior High student, it is time to begin to live your faith out rather than strictly filling yourself up with knowledge. By focusing on one verse weekly, you're given the chance to put into practice what you have been studying. It's up to you to live it out!

How can I apply this lesson to my life?

How can I apply this lesson at school?

Recap Your Thoughts

_____

_____

_____

_____

_____

_____

_____

_____

_____

_____

_____

_____

_____

_____

_____

_____

_____

Attitude Check

Our attitudes, however, are the one thing we always have the ability to control.

Talk to God

_____

_____

_____

_____

_____

_____

_____

_____

_____

_____

_____

_____

_____

_____

A Fully-Loaded Life

REWIND

1. What has God promised me this week?

Keeping It Real

When the servant girl saw him there, she said again to those standing around, "This fellow is one of them." ⁷⁰Again he denied it. After a little while, those standing near said to Peter, "Surely you are one of them, for you are a Galilean."

-Mark 14:69-70

2. Does God have anything for me to obey?

3. Have I done anything that I need forgiveness from God for?

4. What lesson does God want me to remember this week?

Things I do not understand about this chapter...

_____

_____

_____

_____

_____

_____

Recap Your Thoughts

_____
_____
_____
_____
_____
_____
_____
_____
_____
_____
_____
_____
_____

God Listens

God is willing to listen to us; however, we must understand and believe that God's will may be different from our own.

Talk to God

_____
_____
_____
_____
_____
_____
_____
_____
_____
_____
_____
_____

Fully Loaded

Galatians 5:22-24

But the fruit of the Spirit is love, joy, peace, patience, kindness, goodness, faithfulness, [23]gentleness and self-control. Against such things there is no law. [24]Those who belong to Christ Jesus have crucified the sinful nature with its passions and desires.

A Fully-Loaded Life

TRAILER

Over the past eleven weeks you have seen the characteristics that God calls each Christian to obtain and live by. Hopefully you have gained something out of this study, I know I have! My prayer for you is that now you have developed a hunger for studying the scriptures on your own.

In this lesson, we are reviewing all the topics we have discussed over the past eleven weeks. You will be asked to recall major themes from each chapter. The goal is to refresh your mind with the key points that matter, so you can take them with you into your next phase of life! Let's finish this thing.

***Check out Galatians 5:22 and list
"The Fruit of the Spirit" ***

_____   _____
_____   _____
_____   _____
_____   _____
        _____

PREVIEW

- What lessons have been most helpful for you? Why?

First Things First

Beginning with the end in mind helps you think through the purpose of what you want to learn before you actually learn it.

- What is one "real" thing you have learned this semester that you didn't know or had never thought about before?

- Do you think that this study has helped you to better understand the way God wants you to act as a Christian? If so, how? If not, why?

FEATURE PRESENTATION

As you move through this last lesson, ask God to touch your heart in a way He never has before. Ask Him to reveal some final ideas to you that will help you to show your friends Jesus' love, care and compassion. Most of all, ask God to give you a fresh set of eyes to see any new ideas from the previous studies you might have missed.

A Fully-Loaded Life

Today we're looking at **chapters 1-2.**

- What were these chapters about?

Dear friends, do not be surprised at the painful trial you are suffering, as though something strange were happening to you. ¹³But rejoice that you participate in the sufferings of Christ, so that you may be overjoyed when his glory is revealed. ¹⁴If you are insulted because of the name of Christ, you are blessed, for the Spirit of glory and of God rests on you. ¹⁵If you suffer, it should not be as a murderer or thief or any other kind of criminal, or even as a meddler. ¹⁶However, if you suffer as a Christian, do not be ashamed, but praise God that you bear that name.

-1 Peter 4:12-16

- Write out the memory verse for **chapters 1 and 2** in the back of this book on page 226.

- What does the word "love" mean?

- What was the underlying theme in the story of the lost son told by Jesus?

- Read **1 Peter 4:12-16.** If you are a joyful Christian through trials, what kind of example do you set for non-Christians?

- How do you demonstrate God's love to your friends and even to strangers?

- How can you commit to showing Jesus to your friends? How can you commit to staying joyful?

Recap Your Thoughts

_____
_____
_____
_____
_____
_____
_____
_____
_____
_____
_____
_____
_____
_____
_____

Why Pray?

When we pray to God, we are communicating with the most powerful being ever.

- Dustin Heiner

Talk to God

_____
_____
_____
_____
_____
_____
_____
_____
_____
_____
_____
_____
_____
_____

A Fully-Loaded Life

Today we're reviewing **chapters 3-4.**

- What were these chapters about?

Be still before the LORD and wait patiently for him; do not fret when men succeed in their ways, when they carry out their wicked schemes.
⁸ Refrain from anger and turn from wrath; do not fret-it leads only to evil.
⁹ For evil men will be cut off, but those who hope in the LORD will inherit the land.

-Psalm 37:7-9

- Write out the memory verse for **chapters 3 and 4** in the back of this book on page 226.

- Read **Psalm 37:7-9.** What happens to those who are patient and trust in the Lord?

- Read **Luke 9:10-17** on page 52. Why was the crowd of thousands so patient to receive their food? Why were the disciples so impatient?

- Look up **Luke 6:27-36** in your bible. What two things do verses 27 & 28 tell you to do?

- Do you try to avoid messy problems? What is it that keeps you from showing those in need kindness?

Recap Your Thoughts

_____
_____
_____
_____
_____
_____
_____
_____
_____
_____
_____
_____
_____
_____

Adore God

To adore God means to give God authentic praise for His creativity and power over all creation.

Talk to God

_____
_____
_____
_____
_____
_____
_____
_____
_____
_____
_____
_____

A Fully-Loaded Life

Love must be sincere. Hate what is evil; cling to what is good. [10]Be devoted to one another in brotherly love. Honor one another above yourselves. [11]Never be lacking in zeal, but keep your spiritual fervor, serving the Lord. [12]Be joyful in hope, patient in affliction, faithful in prayer. [13]Share with God's people who are in need. Practice hospitality. [14]Bless those who persecute you; bless and do not curse. [15]Rejoice with those who rejoice; mourn with those who mourn. [16]Live in harmony with one another. Do not be proud, but be willing to associate with people of low position. Do not be conceited. [17]Do not repay anyone evil for evil. Be careful to do what is right in the eyes of everybody. [18]If it is possible, as far as it depends on you, live at peace with everyone. [19]Do not take revenge, my friends, but leave room for God's wrath, for it is written: "It is mine to avenge; I will repay," says the Lord. [20]On the contrary: "If your enemy is hungry, feed him; if he is thirsty, give him something to drink. In doing this, you will heap burning coals on his head." [21]Do not be overcome by evil, but overcome evil with good.

-Romans 12:9-21

Day Three

Check out **chapters 5-6**.

- What were these chapters about?

- Write out the memory verse for **chapters 5 and 6** in the back of this book on page 226.

- Read **Romans 12:9-21**. According to this passage, list some ways we can be good to others.

- Is it easier to "do good" to another person if we forgive them of wronging us? How?

- What is the most difficult part of forgiving somebody?

- In your own words, define faithfulness.

- Now list some action steps for yourself regarding how you can become a person whom God and others can rely on. Start with easy ones and move your way up to harder ones.
    a)
    b)
    c)
    d)
    e)

Recap Your Thoughts

_____
_____
_____
_____
_____
_____
_____
_____
_____
_____
_____
_____
_____
_____

Prayer Warrior

It takes a person with an extremely Godly character to live a life of authentic prayer.

Talk to God

_____
_____
_____
_____
_____
_____
_____
_____
_____
_____
_____
_____

A Fully-Loaded Life

Review **chapters 7-8.**

- What were these chapters about?

In the course of time, the king of the Ammonites died, and his son Hanun succeeded him as king. ² David thought, "I will show kindness to Hanun son of Nahash, just as his father showed kindness to me." So David sent a delegation to express his sympathy to Hanun concerning his father. When David's men came to the land of the Ammonites, ³ the Ammonite nobles said to Hanun their lord, "Do you think David is honoring your father by sending men to you to express sympathy? Hasn't David sent them to you to explore the city and spy it out and overthrow it?" ⁴ So Hanun seized David's men, shaved off half of each man's beard, cut off their garments in the middle at the buttocks, and sent them away. ⁵ When David was told about this, he sent messengers to meet the men, for they were greatly humiliated. The king said, "Stay at Jericho till your beards have grown, and then come back."

-2 Samuel 10:1-5

- Write out the memory verse for **chapters 7 and 8** in the back of this book on page 227.

- Read **2 Samuel 10:1-5.** How does David show a gentle heart toward his men who had been humiliated?

- Read **John 8:1-11** on page 126. What are some key points you can learn from Jesus' behavior and His response to both the woman and the Jewish leaders?

- What is self-control? Why is it important for us to have self-control?

- Write out **1 Corinthians 10:13** from page 144.

- How does this verse make you feel?

Recap Your Thoughts

_____
_____
_____
_____
_____
_____
_____
_____
_____
_____
_____
_____
_____

My Direct Line

Prayer is the line we connect to in order for God to give us that extra touch of love.

Talk to God

_____
_____
_____
_____
_____
_____
_____
_____
_____
_____
_____
_____

A Fully-Loaded Life

CREDITS

Review **chapters 9-11.**

- What were these chapters about?

- Write out the memory verse for **chapters 9, 10, and 11** in the back of this book on page 227.

The credits section is designed to help you apply this week's chapter to your life. It can also be used for further discussion in a small group setting.

- Read **Matthew 14:22-32** on page 164. Are you kind of like Peter? Are you putting your trust in Jesus in minor situations, but as major storms start up you don't trust Him?

- Read **Luke 5:1-11** on page 180. Are you like Simon? Is God calling you to fish for your friends? How are you responding?

- What do you plan to do when confronted with a hard decision to stand up for Jesus?

- Looking at the verse, why do you think it was important that you study "the Fruit of the Spirit?"

Recap Your Thoughts

_____
_____
_____
_____
_____
_____
_____
_____
_____
_____
_____
_____

Got Jesus?

God wants
one thing from
you...Your life.

Talk to God

_____
_____
_____
_____
_____
_____
_____
_____
_____
_____
_____
_____

A Fully-Loaded Life

MEMORY VERSE

But the fruit of the Spirit is love, joy, peace, patience, kindness, goodness, faithfulness, [23]gentleness and self-control. Against such things there is no law. [24]Those who belong to Christ Jesus have crucified the sinful nature with its passions and desires.

- Galatians 5:22-24

Living It Out

As a Junior High student, it is time to begin to live your faith out rather than strictly filling yourself up with knowledge. By focusing on one verse weekly, you're given the chance to put into practice what you have been studying. It's up to you to live it out!

How can I apply this lesson to my life?

How can I apply this lesson at school?

Recap Your Thoughts

_____
_____
_____
_____
_____
_____
_____
_____
_____
_____
_____
_____
_____
_____

Fully-Loaded

A fully-loaded
ifle centers on
the reality
that prayer
works.

Talk to God

_____
_____
_____
_____
_____
_____
_____
_____
_____
_____
_____
_____
_____

A Fully-Loaded Life

REWIND

1. What has God promised me this week?

Keeping It Real

Be still before the LORD and wait patiently for him; do not fret when men succeed in their ways, when they carry out their wicked schemes. [8] Refrain from anger and turn from wrath; do not fret-it leads only to evil. [9] For evil men will be cut off, but those who hope in the LORD will inherit the land.

-Psalm 37:7-9

2. Does God have anything for me to obey?

3. Have I done anything that I need forgiveness from God for?

4. What lesson does God want me to remember this week?

Things I do not understand about this chapter...

_____

_____

_____

_____

_____

_____

Recap Your Thoughts

_____
_____
_____
_____
_____
_____
_____
_____
_____
_____
_____
_____
_____
_____

Just Pray

Prayer is the action of engaging your heart with the heart of God.

Talk to God

_____
_____
_____
_____
_____
_____
_____
_____
_____
_____
_____
_____

A FULLY-LOADED LIFE

SEMESTER MEMORY VERSES

A Fully-Loaded Life

Luke 15:32   The Lost Son   Chapter 1

_____
_____
_____

Luke 15:10   The Lost Sheep   Chapter 2

_____
_____
_____

John 6:14   The Hungry Crowd   Chapter 3

_____
_____
_____

Luke 10:27   The Kind Man   Chapter 4

_____
_____
_____

Matthew 18:26-27   Finding the Good in Another   Chapter 5

_____
_____
_____

Matthew 25:21   Show Me The Money   Chapter 6

_____
_____
_____

John 8:7b   **Why Not Stoner Her**   **Chapter 7**

_____
_____
_____

Luke 4:8   **Self What?**   **Chapter 8**

_____
_____
_____

Matthew 14:31   **Drowning in Fear**   **Chapter 9**

_____
_____
_____

Luke 5:10   **The Miraculous Catch**   **Chapter 10**

_____
_____
_____

Mark 14:72   **Deny or Stand Out**   **Chapter 11**

_____
_____
_____

Galatians 5:22-24   **Fully Loaded**   **Chapter 12**

_____
_____
_____

A Fully-Loaded Life

MESSAGE NOTES

A Fully-Loaded Life

The Lost Son

Scripture Passages

_____

_____

_____

_____

Objective One

_____

_____

_____

_____

Objective Two

_____

_____

_____

_____

Objective Three

_____

_____

_____

_____

Debrief

_____

_____

_____

_____

The Lost Sheep

Scripture Passages

_____
_____
_____
_____

Objective One

_____
_____
_____
_____

Objective Two

_____
_____
_____
_____

Objective Three

_____
_____
_____
_____

Debrief

_____
_____
_____
_____

A Fully-Loaded Life

The Hungry Crowd

Scripture Passages

_____

_____

_____

_____

Objective One

_____

_____

_____

_____

Objective Two

_____

_____

_____

_____

Objective Three

_____

_____

_____

_____

Debrief

_____

_____

_____

_____

The Kind Man

Scripture Passages

_____

_____

_____

_____

Objective One

_____

_____

_____

_____

Objective Two

_____

_____

_____

Objective Three

_____

_____

_____

_____

Debrief

_____

_____

_____

_____

Finding The Good

Scripture Passages

_____

_____

_____

_____

Objective One

_____

_____

_____

_____

Objective Two

_____

_____

_____

_____

Objective Three

_____

_____

_____

_____

Debrief

_____

_____

_____

_____

Show Me The Money

Scripture Passages

_____

_____

_____

_____

Objective One

_____

_____

_____

_____

Objective Two

_____

_____

_____

_____

Objective Three

_____

_____

_____

_____

Debrief

_____

_____

_____

_____

Why Not Stone Her?

Scripture Passages

_____
_____
_____
_____

Objective One

_____
_____
_____
_____

Objective Two

_____
_____
_____
_____

Objective Three

_____
_____
_____
_____

Debrief

_____
_____
_____
_____

Self-What?

Scripture Passages

_____
_____
_____
_____

Objective One

_____
_____
_____
_____

Objective Two

_____
_____
_____
_____

Objective Three

_____
_____
_____
_____

Debrief

_____
_____
_____
_____

A Fully-Loaded Life

Drowning in Fear

Scripture Passages

_____

_____

_____

_____

Objective One

_____

_____

_____

_____

Objective Two

_____

_____

_____

_____

Objective Three

_____

_____

_____

_____

Debrief

_____

_____

_____

_____

The Miraculous Catch

Scripture Passages

_____
_____
_____
_____

Objective One

_____
_____
_____
_____

Objective Two

_____
_____
_____
_____

Objective Three

_____
_____
_____
_____

Debrief

_____
_____
_____
_____

A Fully-Loaded Life

Deny or Stand out

Scripture Passages

_____

_____

_____

_____

Objective One

_____

_____

_____

_____

Objective Two

_____

_____

_____

_____

Objective Three

_____

_____

_____

_____

Debrief

_____

_____

_____

_____

_____

Fully-Loaded

Scripture Passages

_____

_____

_____

_____

Objective One

_____

_____

_____

_____

Objective Two

_____

_____

_____

_____

Objective Three

_____

_____

_____

_____

Debrief

_____

_____

_____

_____

Printed in the United States
61355LVS00005B/154-165